The
HOPE
for
AUDACITY

CRITICAL EDUCATION & ETHICS

Barry Kanpol
General Editor

Vol. 1

The Critical Education and Ethics series
is part of the Peter Lang Education list.
Every volume is peer reviewed and meets
the highest quality standards for content and production.

PETER LANG
New York • Washington, D.C./Baltimore • Bern
Frankfurt • Berlin • Brussels • Vienna • Oxford

The
HOPE
for
AUDACITY

Recapturing Optimism *and* Civility *in* Education

Edited by
Terri Jo Swim, Keith Howard, *and* Il-Hee Kim

PETER LANG
New York • Washington, D.C./Baltimore • Bern
Frankfurt • Berlin • Brussels • Vienna • Oxford

#7788277662

Library of Congress Cataloging-in-Publication Data

The hope for audacity: recapturing optimism and civility in education /
edited by Terri Jo Swim, Keith Howard, Il-Hee Kim.
pages cm. — (Critical education and ethics; vol. 1)
Includes bibliographical references.
1. Education—United States. 2. Effective teaching—United States.
3. Public schools—United States. I. Swim, Terri Jo.
II. Howard, Keith. III. Kim, Il-Hee.
LA217.2.H66   370.973—dc23   2012005437
ISBN 978-1-4331-1853-1 (hardcover)
ISBN 978-1-4331-1852-4 (paperback)
ISBN 978-1-4539-0775-7 (e-book)
ISSN 2166-1359

Bibliographic information published by **Die Deutsche Nationalbibliothek**.
Die Deutsche Nationalbibliothek lists this publication in the "Deutsche
Nationalbibliografie"; detailed bibliographic data is available
on the Internet at http://dnb.d-nb.de/.

The paper in this book meets the guidelines for permanence and durability
of the Committee on Production Guidelines for Book Longevity
of the Council of Library Resources.

© 2012 Peter Lang Publishing, Inc., New York
29 Broadway, 18th floor, New York, NY 10006
www.peterlang.com

Printed in the United States of America

This book is dedicated to all the children and families who feel like they are being left behind by our current educational policies and practices.

Contents

Part III: Overview

Conclusion

Acknowledgments

The three editors would like to thank Barry Kanpol, Series Editor, for his visions and to Dawn Adams, our secretary, for her patience and careful attention to detail during the manuscript preparation.

T.S., K.H., & I.K.

I would like to thank my husband, Danny, for his enduring support and to my children, Savannah, Randy, and Justin for sharing their perspectives on educational issues.

T. S.

I would like to thank my wife, Nicol, for her patience and unequivocal support, and to my children, Dwan, Imani, Micaela, and Kamau, for being an endless source of inspiration.

K.H.

I would like to thank my wife, Eunju Yoon, for her constant support and love for me.

I.K.

Foreword

Terri Jo Swim, Keith Howard,
& Il-Hee Kim

"Hope is like a road in the country; there was never a road, but when many people walk on it, the road comes into existence."

—Lin Yutang

"If you lose hope, somehow you lose the vitality that keeps life moving, you lose that courage to be, that quality that helps you go on in spite of it all. And so today I still have a dream."

—Martin Luther King, Jr.

In the realm of public education, we must have the vision and courage to dream of new possibilities, follow the road less traveled, and even, at times, pave new roads into the future. For far too long, public education was under the shadow of terms such as *failing schools*, *achievement gaps*, and *poor classroom management*. To "cure" these ailments, the No Child Left Behind (NCLB) Act was enacted in 2001. However, far from representing a cure, the law has resulted in schools, teachers, and, most important, children thinking that their worth is based entirely on one score on a standardized test and has generated more controversies and issues. Although many, many publications have outlined the problems and consequences of NCLB, this is not the intent of this book. Our goal is to capture our power, collectively and individually, to illuminate our hopes and dreams for pubic education.

We feel that the time is right for sharing our hopes for the future due to the historical event we have experienced: the election of Barack Obama as president of the United States of America. This election signified for many citizens a change in direction for the country, a hope for a better future, and a break from the past ways of "doing business" in Washington, DC. The president himself has reminded citizens of the power of hope and how the audacity to hope can lead the nation forward (Obama, 2006).

Responding to President Obama's educational policies and practices to lead the field forward, education faculty from two institutions—one in the Midwest (Indiana University-Purdue University Fort Wayne [IPFW]) and the other on the West Coast (Chapman University)—have collaborated on writing projects, which have culminated in a trilogy of books. The authors in this first installment of the trilogy articulate their hopes for public education through raising critical questions for discussion. This book is not about despair. Rather, it is about paving roads that will make the hope for a better future a reality. As Singh and Han (2007) noted, we believe that hope is the source of motivation for new scientific inventions and innovative solutions to social problems; it provides bold imaginings of what might be grounded in rigorous verification.

For the authors of this book, having the audacity to hope for better public education means trusting teachers and children to engage in intellectual endeavors that advocate for the development of the whole person and active participation in a democratic community. Each of the authors approaches the task of bringing the hope to reality in their own unique way. Our hope is that the collection of ideas and approaches, woven with the same threads of optimism and determination that captured much of the nation during the campaign leading to Obama's presidency, can help to illuminate the opportunities that the present circumstances provide. At the same time, we realize that no single approach addressed in this book, or even this collection of ideas in its entirety, will address all of the challenges that we are faced with as a nation. The problems are too multifaceted and complex. The president himself struggles with contradictions within his own policies. For example, he strongly believes in the importance of competition to improve teacher performance and accountability (e.g., the Race to the Top initiative). However, he wants teachers held in high esteem like in some Asian countries (e.g., South Korea). He states,

> Here in America, it's time we treated the people who educate our children with the same level of respect. We want to reward good teachers and stop making excuses for bad ones. And over the next 10 years, with so many baby boomers retiring from our classrooms, we want to prepare 100,000 new teachers in the fields of science and technology and engineering and math. (Obama, 2011, ¶ 37)

Preparing teachers for the challenges and rewards of the 21st century will not be easy. It will take intentional partnerships among higher education faculty, administrators, practicing teachers, and state/federal government officials. People on both sides of the aisle believe that there is hope for our children's education, and we hold that joint outcomes cannot be achieved through coercion, mandates, or contests. We cannot work against one another or walk different paths. We humbly assert that we must forge a new road together. If we continue to have these important conversations with the right combination of vigor, tenor, and compassion, we can harness the enormous energy and achieve our common goal of providing our nation's children with the opportunity to achieve the best education they can get. But how do we forge such new pathways with civility when there are so many different perspectives, agenda, and egos, both individually and collectively, that may complicate the process?

The Introduction, written by Barry Kanpol, presents one of the pathways for achieving the goal. He suggests that the notion of reskilling gives us hope for the future. The theoretical perspective of deskilling and reskilling provides a framework for viewing our history and future as a profession. He brings this framework to life with empirically based examples of how certain conditions within schools can profoundly affect the learning outcomes that result. Kanpol illuminates the impact that others-directed instruction can have on the level of academic freedom that teachers are allowed to bring to the task of educating children. It provides the kind of insight often missing in the public discourse on the problems in our educational system. It is perfectly understandable when political leaders and others outside of education look at achievement numbers in a vacuum and conclude that something must change in the way teachers do their jobs in the classroom. However, when teachers are given the opportunity to provide noneducators with a glimpse into the not so cut-and-dry realities of the classroom experience, we may find less advocacy for simple solutions to solve what are increasingly complex problems. Adding more tests, longer hours, and higher stakes to the education palette sounds promising if one remains convinced that the main problems are effort and accountability alone. A very different approach may emerge if we were to find that large numbers of teachers and students genuinely want to be successful but are in need of practical approaches to accomplish this goal.

The chapters in Part I address the educational issues of unintended consequences and rights of children. The chapters in Parts II and III provide specific examples of how teachers can be reskilled, as suggested in the

Introduction. A more detailed overview of each chapter is provided at the beginning of each part.

The book concludes by highlighting the theme—civility—which is woven throughout the chapters of this book. Alice Merz and Terri Swim take this collection of perspectives and respond to the question, Where do we go from here? They identify the challenge that is before us and call on us to bring audacity to bear on an endeavor that is as important as anything we can imagine. With the right commitment, compassion, vision, and leadership, greatness is within our reach.

At the beginning, we stated that the ushering in of change was welcomed with the new administration. There was hope that one change in the system would help spur another change. In this book, we try not to point a finger at any one group: teachers, politicians, unions, parents, or children. We instead acknowledge the complexity for all. It is the system as a whole that needs to continue developing. We have robust hope that by expanding the conversation about educational policies and practices, we can harness our collective power to reskill teachers and children by forging new pathways.

—*Terri Jo Swim, IPFW*
Keith Howard, Chapman University
Il-Hee Kim, IPFW

References

Obama, B. (2006). *The audacity of hope: Thoughts on reclaiming the American dream.* New York: Vintage Books.

———. (2011). *State of the Union Address.* Available at http://www.huffingtonpost.com/2011/01/25/obama-state-of-the-union-_1_n_813478.html.

Singh, M., & Han, S. (2007). Making hope robust in teacher education. *Asia-Pacific Journal of Teacher Education, 35*(3), 223–225.

Mr. President: The Time Has Come to Reskill Our Teaching Force, So Please, Please, Let's Get Real!

Barry Kanpol

Mr. President:

I start this chapter with a note to you, Mr. President. As I do so, I realize that I am straying from traditional academic structures of manuscript for publication writing. I will surely return to them, however, as that is my comfort zone. But a far more critical issue for me is that I, like many others in this book and in this trilogy of books on educational issues published by Peter Lang Publishing, also believe quite firmly that you too need to stray from traditional policy measures in educational issues to help make inroads into the enormous disparities facing our country on educational matters, particularly as they relate to race, class, and gender concerns. I come to the table also realizing that as a former high school teacher, university faculty member, chair of a department, and now dean of a School of Education, where we predominantly prepare teachers and leaders for public schools, I have been writing about the issues I will present shortly for close to 25 years. Mr. President, I feel a strong conviction about my ideas, none of which is original, but many of which are shared by a broad array of scholars. I humbly ask that you give them a read and, in doing so, perhaps open a dialogue with me (us) over some of the concerns we have in this book. In a more traditional form, I want to elaborate on two theoretical concepts that are central to the accountability models you have both engineered and solidified in this country: a simple reinforcing of the Reagan, Bush, Clinton, and Bush eras that preceded you. Those concepts are deskilling and reskilling. I then present snippets of data from three case studies that show why a movement away from strict accountability models is essential to a solid education. I then analyze the data with that point in mind. In my conclusions to you, in note form again, I respectfully ask you to consider alternative methods to the ones you have had Secretary Duncan and his troops impose.

Deskilling Versus Reskilling

Within a traditional school setting, it has been argued, time and again, that teachers' skills have been slowly eroded. A history of empirical work (Apple & Teitlebaum, 1986; Bullough, Gitlin, & Goldstein, 1984) depicts how teacher work is reduced mainly to its technical aspects, as in the application of rules and, for the most part, the exclusion of teachers from curriculum-making processes. Here, teachers lose control over their own labor, allowing outside forces to manage their work. Deskilling has to do with teachers executing someone else's goals and plans. In industry, this is referred to as the separation of conception from execution (Apple, 1986, 1996; Braverman, 1974). In schools, this appears as well and has been greatly supported and reinforced with No Child Left Behind (NCLB) and Race to the Top (RTTT) forces of accountability control. It seems to me that deskilling is at its peak when teachers are denied or have much less autonomy and less control over the teaching process than they think they have. By making teachers accountable for federal- and state-mandated curriculum and by promoting competency-based education, system management, and the employment of rigid and dehumanizing forms of evaluation along with numerical rating scales and well-crafted rubrics, teachers are controlled and simply march to the tune of the state, with little or no input as to what counts as sound teaching or a good education.

Nothing disturbs me more than visiting my children's schools and hearing teachers emotionally respond in despairing and authentic ways to their inability to teach creatively. Rather, they are forced to teach to the state-mandated test (in Indiana—ISTEP) without any professional input! Critics (Kumashiro, 2009) have argued that the carrying out of recent reforms and the promotion of someone like Arne Duncan to lead our country in educational matters simply exacerbate the alienation, oppression, and subordination of teachers to the will of the state despite Duncan's so-called successes as defined by the removal of the bottom echelon of low-achieving schools from his home city (Giroux, 2010; Giroux & Saltman, 2010). The competition is on. Teachers now have to think about their students passing a state-mandated test to either keep their jobs or save the school from a state corporate-like takeover. Rather than educating our future leaders, we are told to manage and control bits of knowledge that, in my estimation, many children and even teachers at times find quite useless. Dewey (1938) was correct to argue that education must be relevant for the child and that there must be a connection between the curriculum and interest, and the child and experience for optimum achievement results as well as student interest to occur. In schools, I am sure that you, Mr. President, as well as Mr. Duncan, understand that much more occurs than simply knowledge control. The much-used term *hidden curriculum* teaches us that issues of race, class, and gender are connected to curricula issues. It teaches us that learning occurs in the hallways, in the streets, on the playground, and on the busses. I once visited a hard-hit middle school in Compton, California. The eighth-grade class I attended had 50 students with the seventh teacher that year! There were two pregnant girls. No state-mandated curriculum could replace the joy that this teacher had in taking kids out to the playground and teaching facts relevant to the kids' lives, making noises and different smells with the Bunsen burner, and simply trying to reach kids where they were.

In summary, deskilling occurs when the efficiency and mastery of content are taken out of teacher control and placed in the hands of state bureaucrats. This occurs without considering vast human differences, particularly as related to different ethnicities. These arguments are not to say that teachers should NOT be held accountable for student success. It would be foolish of me to argue against some form of teacher accountability. What I am suggesting, however, is to expand on the notion of what teachers can do by not ONLY limiting them to rigid accountability measures. I turn to the notion of reskilling to further these arguments.

A move away from deskilling occurs when teachers are able to better intellectualize the role the state plays in constructing knowledge and subsequently curriculum. Today, teachers are more aware of state intrusions than ever before. As mentioned, frustration levels are at a historical high, as is student cynicism and apathy, while teacher morale is at a historically low ebb. Teachers are simply attuned to the fact that they no longer make curriculum decisions, must seriously teach to the state-mandated test, and have no control over policy concerns. Reskilling, I argue, occurs when teachers have more control over their own labor. Time and again, the president has argued that it is the community (Obama, 2005, 2006, 2007, 2008) that matters. To me, communities differ and so, by definition, must the school curriculum. Not all school communities can perform at the same state- or federal-mandated level, particularly as arguments have been correctly made that standardized tests are skewed to average and high achievers as well as privileged school communities (Kohn, 2000). Reskilling occurs when the curriculum is connected to who kids are, their subjectivities, and their likes and dislikes. Reskilling occurs when the curriculum is connected to a broad knowledge base that links to multiple learning styles. In my own case, for instance, I dropped out of high school. All kids were expected to learn the same way; memorize, regurgitate, and reproduce. Some students are visual learners, whereas others are not. I didn't fit the system that customized a particular type of student. Surely reskilling takes into consideration that knowledge is gained differently. Surely a standardized curriculum needs to be linked to how kids learn and perform and under what conditions—economic and social. Clearly, it is far easier to deskill teachers and students than to reskill them. To reskill takes an intimate look at the social dynamics of the classroom as a priority and as a necessary condition to build curriculum rather than build curriculum first and worry about these social dynamics later. I turn to the classroom now with three snippets of data to view how reskilling may occur in a practical sense. Although these snippets of data occurred years ago, they still symbolically represent many of the goings on in schools today.

Study 1

Four eighth-grade teachers were studied at Hillview Middle School (Kanpol, 1999).[1] One emerging theme in this study was the teachers' consistent refusal to teach to a state-mandated curriculum. In part, this happened because (a) students in this working-class school were not reaching the eighth-grade level of state-mandated standardized curriculum objectives, and (b) some teachers prioritized social issues as a pragmatic curriculum in the classroom, a form of reskilling. This deviated from the more objective, state-mandated, deskilled curriculum. Two examples illustrate this point.

Using eighth-grade reading materials to teach children who had third-grade reading skills seemed an impossible task and had to be dealt with pragmatically. Third-grade literature needed to be used. Ms. A told her students that she would let them relax and read different types of literature. Thus, her eighth-grade students talked about time, characterization, and place as part of the official curriculum in *Sylvester and the Magic Pebble* (not in the official state-mandated curriculum). Students immersed themselves in the newer, spontaneous curriculum. Ms. A noted:

> Now I can do more creative-type, pragmatic activities with my students rather than boring exercises in the regular curriculum....We openly talk about things like drugs....I decided that students gained nothing by doing exercises made by the other teacher and even less by following a curriculum that is not on their traditional levels.

A student responded to Ms. A's curriculum:

> She lets us do things the other teachers don't. We don't take dumb tests....She's good, lets us read what we want.

Ms. Y, the eighth-grade social studies teacher and "activist" outside and inside the school among the eighth-grade teachers, raised the complex issues of race and prejudice with her students and used this as part of her curriculum. In part, this was the result of a sexual assault issue at the school through which Ms. Y and Ms. A were persuaded to challenge the school administration's handling of the situation. The issue of gender rights became the central concern for these teachers. This was based on their caring qualities. In some ways, the sexual assault issues led Ms. Y to modify her standards-based curriculum. While the official curriculum, state mandated, dealt with facts, the hidden and reskilled curriculum dealt with far broader and life-changing instances. After watching the movie *Mask*, Ms. Y asks students about prejudice:

St. (1): I guess, well, we all have a few prejudices, I mean um, do we like everything, um and everyone in this school?

Ms. Y: What are some of your prejudices?

Ms. Y: What makes you better?

St. (2): He's not better. He's the same. We are all the same, just do things differently.

Ms. Y's reskilled and hidden curriculum was concerned with the rights of students to be treated equally. Often a standardized curriculum, built for test taking, cannot deviate. So much is obviously missed out on. In short, what emerges from Ms. A and Ms. Y's use of technically lower reading material for eighth-grade students is the promotion of both self-esteem and voice for individual students, certainly a form of reskilling, and in some ways revamped curriculum that links official aspects to broad social concerns.

Study 2

One teacher was studied at Parkview Elementary School (Kanpol, 1999). My central concern was to determine how Betty, a fourth-grade teacher, would incorporate a global perspective into her daily social studies curriculum even though global education (the cross-cultural study and awareness of both problems and issues concerning the economic, political, environmental, cultural, and technological aspects of other countries) had not yet been standardized.

Officially, Betty was supposed to follow the Instructional Television Program (ITV) for social studies purposes. Heavy reliance on ITV for art, music, and social studies, combined with a top-down decision structure in the school district, suggests that the deskilling of teachers was occurring in this particular district. However, as an act of resistance to this form of deskilling, Betty created curriculum autonomy for herself. She decided to create a 3-week unit about different countries in order to help students learn about individual and cultural differences. Asked why she used this curriculum, Betty commented:

> Some prejudices that I experienced made me want to know what others were like and why there's discrimination and so on. Our regular curriculum doesn't go into that stuff.

Concerning her use of a more practical curriculum, Betty said:

> The ITV is just the tip of the iceberg. The real teaching comes when I connect peoples of the world with the ecology movement, for example. I will do more simulations that could be more political. For instance, we will learn about some countries' hunger problems, and why we must do away with that. At the same time, while we work on these ideas, we do them in groups, for the experiences of working together and sharing ideas, accepting and understanding different points of view, just being a community.

I observed how a 3-week global education project evolved and became a group shared activity. The emerging themes of understanding different points of view, building empathy, creating community, and resisting individualism predominated in Betty's hidden and pragmatic curriculum. In a class exercise designed to introduce students to the notion of difference, Betty placed a number of items on a round table at the front of the class. The students listed everything they saw from where they were seated. After 5 minutes, the class came together to talk about what they had seen.

Betty:	What did you discover?
St. (1):	I can't see from a distance.
St. (2):	That nobody's perfect.
Betty:	Would you like to have a perfect list? How would you feel about not seeing everything? Go about it? Upset?
St. (1):	Upset. Cheated because some people saw different things and we were all sitting at different places.
Betty:	What would you have wished you had done?
St. (3):	I felt mistreated.
St. (4):	How could you get all the information?
St. (5):	Look for different points of view.
Betty:	How many points of view are there?
St. (6):	Many, at least two. You can see different things if you stand in different places.
Betty:	Can you see everything when you are real close?
Students:	Yeah.
Betty:	What can you tell me about your point of view? What can change your point of view?
St. (1):	When you look different.
Betty:	If I put more makeup on or dress differently, does that change your point of view?

In all, Betty taught that members of different groups have different points of view and that people in different countries have different customs and habits. The standardized curriculum never emphasized differences or allowed teachers to deviate or reskill themselves and their students. Although this study was conducted well before the onset of NCLB, admittedly this teacher had more freedom to experiment with her curriculum. What is obvious is the difference it can make when creativity reigns and the curriculum is not controlled top down. The 3-week unit plan, of which just a snippet was included, symbolized a move from an official ITV curriculum to a pragmatic, creative, and reskilled unit plan designed for students to become literate about each other, themselves, and the outside world. Good teaching, in short!

Study 3

Five teachers were studied at Chapel High School (Kanpol, 1999). I chose to look at Sarah's pedagogy, one that like others in the study dealt with gender, empathy, differences, inequities, and understanding others. Oftentimes this pragmatic and reskilled curriculum took precedence over the officially mandated curriculum.

Sarah, a native-born Egyptian, is also an English as a Second Language (ESL) teacher. She stringently followed the official curriculum guidelines and used suggested texts. However, she did not believe that curriculum ends with official texts. To the contrary, Sarah commented that her "other curriculum is her interaction with students both in and out of the class." In a discussion on the concept of "home," related directly to the poem, "All Alone," which was read aloud in class, she said to the students:

> Let me share something with you now that you are just new immigrants. A home is never the same once you leave it. Finding a new home is like transplanting a plant. This is what happened to me when I left Egypt. Everything would look different to me. It doesn't mean you are going to be different. Don't forget your good qualities. Choose the good things America has to offer. Then you'll be unique. This is how I feel. Just because you are different doesn't make you worse. We are richer because of our differences.

This deviation from the official curriculum as a way to penetrate her students' feelings and thought structures was further amplified in a discussion on conflict based on an official text for this ESL class, *The Lady or the Tiger*.

Sarah, who believes that conflict must be related to students' personal lives, commented:

> I give them a conflict situation before we read on conflict such as if we have a small house or my two ways of solving conflict—fight or flight. So I say it's better to work things out and fight out conflict. They have many of the same conflicts as when I came from Egypt. I am a role model for them. I also suffered just like these kids. I was in a similar situation—had to make a choice—fight or flight. I know what they went through. I interrelated personal conflict with the general conflict they face every day. As immigrants they will always have these conflicts.

Much of the official curriculum that Sarah chose had to do with potential conflict situations. The following discussion is based on *The Lady or the Tiger*:

Sarah:	What is the meaning of conflict?
St. (1):	A problem.
Sarah:	A problem that arises from what?
St. (2):	A difficult situation.
Sarah:	Very good. There's one thing very important about this story. What is it?
St. (3):	She's an individual.
St. (4):	She's independent.
Sarah:	Oh, wonderful, yes, she did what she wanted. She was disobedient to her father.
St. (3):	The king didn't approve of the relationship…his daughter and the slave.
Sarah:	So, what conflict do we have here?
St. (5):	Inner conflict.

Students were beginning to understand the nature of inner conflict. A week later, Sarah connected this understanding to theory:

Sarah:	What is theory?
St. (1):	An idea.
Sarah:	Is the idea always correct?
St. (6):	No!
Sarah:	Yes, someone has to prove it right or wrong. Let's see, Christopher Columbus had a theory.
St. (7):	Yes, the world goes round.
Sarah:	Did people believe him?
St. (8):	Not everyone.
Sarah:	Then we have a conflict between what's right and what's wrong.

It is clear from the snippets of these case studies that teachers are much more than mere technicians or deskilled practitioners—simple minded, narrow, and efficient, only concerned with and committed to the official and mandated curriculum. Thinking teachers, like the ones just described, are faced with and are symbolic of enormous struggles in our schools. For the most part, they teach what the state says to but struggle mightily on a daily basis with the humane and dignified aspect of teaching to the "whole" child, to where the child is at in his or her life, to the social situation, and to the experiences and conundrums that children face in their daily lives. I expand on more emerging themes in the next section.

Emerging Themes

Around the concept of reskilling lie the interrated concepts of voice and, ultimately, similarity within difference. It has been argued elsewhere (McLaren, 1989) that the concept of voice is central to a notion of reskilling teachers and students. First, voice is meaningful dialogue. Second, voice is the internalized and private conversation shaped by one's history and self. In the previous cases, voice is used by both students and teachers to interpret personal experiences, in particular as related to one's own oppression, subordination, and alienation. Third, a more abstract notion of voice shapes power structures within schools. We can understand voice when we view how cultural artifacts such as dress, language, history, stereotype, race, and gender make up diverse school cultures and when we discern how these artifacts symbolize the often hierarchical teacher–student and teacher–teacher relationships.

As teachers personalize the curriculum, they reskill themselves and students when moving from an official to a pragmatic one, from unquestioned acceptance of information to a critical view of knowledge construction. For example, Ms. Y seriously questioned student prejudices. This became the basis of students' race and gender reflections, much similar to the current president's in his books as he talks about race relationships. Ms. A created a newer and more spontaneous curriculum that allowed students to understand their sense of voice, which included the understanding of their time, characterization, and place. Betty insisted on reskilling herself and students around issues of difference, one centered on tolerance, empathy, and care. Sarah had students question authority, if nothing else, so as to solve conflicts. Her message was that students can come together through similarities despite differences. Yes, similarity of stereotype experiences and feelings of alienation would bind teachers and students despite individual differences.

With this in mind, there may be many reasons for deviations from the official curriculum, such as time constraints, boredom with the curriculum and student and teacher apathy, as well as teachers simply being fed up with state interventions. It is also clear that all of the teachers where these studies were conducted and a far greater number of teachers I visit in schools today are not only dissatisfied with, but professionally abhor the top-down official curriculum as truth with a capital T. They are also disgruntled with the incessant testing that takes place as a result of a competitive and growing market logic imposed nationally over the last 20 years or so, more so the last few years.

It is through creating a new curriculum, albeit an unofficial pragmatic one, that teachers are reskilled within the severe boundaries of the limitations they face. These teachers cannot simply be depicted as only storers and dis-seminators of bits of knowledge who develop narrow basic skills to be taught in a standardized kind of way. Rather, these teachers are attempting to find a meaningful bridge between the official aspects of the deskilled curriculum and a new creative area where they can authentically educate students, which results in forms of reskilling.

Mr. President:

I now return to my lesser comfort zone…a conclusion that talks to you in-stead of the kind of academic conclusion expected of me. I symbolically stood by you as you pronounced, "Yes we can." I read your books and linked your ethnic struggles to mine (a chapter in another book of this trilogy), your differences to mine, and your issues of leadership (albeit quite different) to mine. I intuitively understand that I simply cannot put myself in the shoes of my superiors and, for sure, not your shoes. From your vantage point, howev-er, it must be excruciatingly difficult to believe in the core of the American Dream of a fair shot for all and yet impose what seems to be a contradictory top-down model of corporate efficiency for our schools, particularly under Mr. Duncan's leadership. I still believe in you, Mr. President. You see, I choose to believe that, despite your privileged education and seeming com-mitment to community politics and local control in our communities, you would be bothered greatly by a curriculum that is so high stakes oriented and clearly created for the middle American that you may have lost sight of your own history! Mr. President, I choose to believe that you would be perturbed by teachers who are more bored than ever in the history of their/our great profession. Mr. President, I choose to believe that you are still bothered by comments such as my son makes on how irrelevant the information he re-ceives from his daily goings on at school, to his experiences, to what his cre-ative and whole self could be if schools were different! Mr. President, I choose to believe that you really do care about this age-old profession of ours, one that is engaged in a cultural war of trying to educate kids rather than produce robots. I know I didn't succeed in that particular system. I know you struggled with it. Mr. President, wouldn't you like your children and grandchildren to have teachers like Betty, Ms. Y, and Sarah, for example, teachers who stray from the corporate curriculum to challenge children in questioning their identity? Mr. President, both you and I know that schools are fundamental to the survival of our democracy. I hope we can both agree that at least one role of schools is to produce a critical citizenry, rather than a citizenry that goes to the voting booths but only votes based on hearsay and an uneducated and mechanical view of the world. For that is what deskilling does, Mr. President. It limits us. It controls us. It seeks to silence us.

Mr. President, many of the chapters in this book talk in some way or another about the deskilling process. Some chapters also talk about or deal with reskilling, albeit in different ways than this chapter. This particular chapter, however, has provided you with an avenue to see how, through understanding student voice, the curriculum can be viewed as a form of reskilling. I invite you to our dialogue in the hope that we indeed can create an authentic community dialogue as well as a systematic and practical agenda of transformative change that is not deskilled or corporate based. I still choose to believe, Mr. President. I hope you do, too.

Notes

Introduction

1.   All names of teachers and students are pseudonyms.

References

Apple, M. (1996). *Cultural politics and education.* New York: Teachers College Press.

———. (1986). *Teachers and texts.* New York: Routledge & Kegan Paul.

Apple, M., & Teitlebaum, K. (1986). Are teachers losing control of their skills and curriculum? *Journal of Curriculum Studies, 18*(3), 177–184.

Braverman, H. (1974). *Labor and monopoly capital.* New York: Monthly Review Press.

Bullough, R., Gitlin, A., & Goldstein, A. (1984). Ideology, teacher role and resistance. *Teacher's College Record, 87,* 219–237.

Dewey, J. (1938). *Experience and education.* New York: Collier Macmillan Publishers.

Giroux, H. (2010). Challenging the military-industrial-academic complex after 9/11. *Policy Futures in Education, 8*(2), 232–237.

Giroux, H., & Saltman, K. (2010). *Obama's betrayal of public education: Arne Duncan and the corporate model of schooling.* Available at http:/www.truthout.org//121708R?print

Kanpol, B. (1999). *Critical pedagogy: An introduction.* Westport, CT: Bergin & Garvey.

Kohn, A. (2000). *The schools our children deserve: Moving beyond traditional classrooms and "tougher standards."* New York: Houghton Mifflin Company.

Kumashiro, K. (2009, January 12). Wrong choice for secretary of education: A dissenting voice from Chicago. *Education Week.* Available at http://www.edweek.org/ew/articles/2009/01/12/18kumashiro-com.h28.html

McLaren, P. (1989). *Life in schools.* New York: Longman.

Obama, B. (2005, October 25). *Teaching our kids in a 21st century economy.* Speech delivered to the Center for American Progress. Available at http://obama.senate.gov/speech/05105-teaching_our_ki/

———. (2006). *The audacity of hope: Thoughts on reclaiming the American dream.* New York: Random House, Inc.

———. (2007, November 20). *Our kids, our future.* Speech delivered in Manchester, NH. Available at http://www.barackobama.com2007/11/20/remarks_of_senator_barack_obama_34.php

———. (2008, May 28). *What's possible for our children.* Speech delivered in Thornton, CO. Available at http://www.denverpost.com/news/ci_9405199

PART I

Overview

The two chapters that follow (Chapters 1 and 2) address issues linked to policies and the reform efforts underway to improve the quality of public education. In "Expanding the Realm," Chris Strople (Chapter 1) provides a look at some of the unintended consequences that can result when a narrow focus on standardized testing as the only measure of excellence in education becomes systemic. Well-intentioned administrators, like many political leaders, sometimes miss the mark when the only thing that seems to matter is test results. Many administrators and teachers find themselves under pressure to make their projected annual yearly progress and stay away from NCLB sanctions, all while dealing with overcrowded classrooms and schools. Strople shows us how this indirect deskilling of teachers and administrators creates a narrow focus on test scores, which can result in less attention and resources being directed toward caring initiatives that may positively affect those same test outcomes. In so doing, he reminds us that the education of children is as much a human act of caring as it is a method of securing predetermined achievement outcomes. He asks us to examine the purpose of our legislation through a different lens, one that argues for more time and space in the everyday duties of school operations to care about the individuals who we say we are there to serve.

In Chapter 2, Ben Mardell, Lisa Fiore, Marina Boni, and Melissa Tonachel continue the policy and reform discussion addressing the impact that our affinity for increased testing has on the very youngest of students in public education. Their chapter, "The Rights of Children: Policies to Best Serve 3-, 4-, and 5-Year-Olds in Public Schools," describes the impact that teachers and administrators have on children's values toward education and what they perceive to be quality education. The observed shift to a business model can result in changes in our approaches to preparing preschoolers, which include specific preparation for their eventual entry into the testing frenzy that will occur throughout their K-12 experience. The authors warn us of the possible ramifications of this shifting focus, which amounts to a deskilling of our early educators in a way that contradicts their natural nurturing instincts. The shift takes them from constructivist approaches that feed the natural curiosity of young children to a means-end approach that can stifle the inquisitiveness that is essential in maintaining a love for learning. By reskilling these teachers with greater support and a commitment to making a caring environment a non-negotiable element of their classrooms, we can preserve the optimism and hope that many of our students come to school with. In so doing, we can reignite the hope that inspired so many educators as the Obama administration began.

Expanding the Realm

Chris Strople

This chapter strives to provide some information and insight about public education in the United States today. Some of this you will have undoubtedly heard before. Some of this, however, comes from my experiences as a teacher for more than a decade in public school classrooms. This chapter is also about assumptions, some of them simple and some of them complex. These assumptions often emerge from both the practice of education and the policy that guides it. Some of the less complicated assumptions include an insistence (some would say a right, even if it is not explicitly stated in the Constitution) that all children receive a free and appropriate education; some of the more complex include how an equal education, although claimed to be an opportunity afforded to all children, is much more difficult to actualize.

One of the objectives of this chapter is to provide something of value to as he considers future policy and practice for public education in the United States. I would like to assume that you, Mr. President, will take the time to read this. I could base this assumption on some of the knowledge that I have gathered about you. For instance, I know that you have a habit of reading letters from citizens in the evening when you are working on important matters of state. I also know that you have authored two books (both of which I have read, by the way), so perhaps you would enjoy reading a book or two specifically addressed to you.

Another objective of this chapter is to discuss the act of caring, its role in education and in policy, and also how assumptions about caring can lead to unintended consequences. This discussion relies heavily on evidence gathered from experience; experience shared from the perspective of a student as she navigated through a public school system derived from current education policy, from her family as they interacted with her and that system, and from a teacher who worked within that system for more than a decade.

The thing is, I really wouldn't know if you read this unless you told me so. That would be evidence. It is evidence that we strive for when considering assumptions so that we may more clearly apprehend a situation or an occurrence. So the following is, in part, about assumptions and, in equal part, about evidence. The hope here is to discuss some of the particulars of these assumptions to facilitate a better understanding of the evidence.

Policy and Practice

Who sets public education policy? Who provides the insight during its formation, and how is it that this insight can be drafted into something both intelligible and accessible? Starting with questions may appear a bit elementary especially when there is an urgent need for a solution. It seems to me that asking questions and asking them repeatedly can be vital to the consideration of an answer. Learning often begins with questions, and so much of our knowledge originated from the asking of questions. These questions and their subsequent explorations help to guard against assumptions that would otherwise take their place. In the public dialogue, there are assumptions about what public education is or what it should be, and yet these assumptions are often out of touch with the evidence that we have. An example would be the current federal policy regarding public education in the United States.

There is usually at least one degree of separation from an idea and its application, and often more than one. Extending that statement to policy and its practice is simple enough, and the assumption is that practice will follow policy with minimal interference. Policy decisions (both legislative and judicial) regarding public education in the United States, such as *Brown v. Board of Education* in *1954 (Brown)*, the Elementary and Secondary Education Act (ESEA) of 1965, the Individuals with Disabilities Education Act (IDEA) of 1990, the Improving America's Schools Act (IASA) of 1994, the No Child Left Behind Act (NCLB) of 2001, and, most recently, *A Blueprint for Reform (Blueprint) of 2010*, have attempted to guide practice so that the ideas encapsulated within those policies would be applied for the benefit of all. However, the historical reality provides evidence that is not always consistent with the historical idealism of those policies.

The emphasis on research-based data to enhance policymaking for public education is largely a step in the right direction for schools, public education, and society. Without research, assumption can dominate the dialogue of policy, and public education runs the risk of being subjected to whim and fancy, fads and trends. Research provides the opportunity to more clearly comprehend the complexities prevalent in education. Research also affords the possibility of discerning the evidence so that public policy will be shaped to better meet the needs of the public.

Of course the assumption here is that all those conducting and reviewing the research are doing so with the needs of the public forefront in their consideration of such evidence. The No Child Left Behind (NCLB) Act of 2001 is an apt example of this assumption. The stated objective of this act is, "To close the achievement gap with accountability, flexibility, and choice, so that no child is left behind" (No Child Left Behind, 20 U.S.C. § 1). One of the ways that the objective of this act is measured is by the use of standardized tests. These standardized tests provide both data and research about those accumulated data as evidence of whether this objective is being met and whether the policy that has instituted the practice in public education of leaving no child behind is adequately meeting the needs of the public.

What is the purpose of public education today? Is the purpose to provide all children, all future citizens, with an education? If so, what is this education comprised of? Reading, writing, and arithmetic perhaps? Do all of our children deserve this education, and if so will they all have equal access and opportunity? At first glance, these questions all appear easily answered. Yes, the purpose of public education is to provide all children with equal access and opportunity to a quality education that will include language arts and math. Yes, all of our children deserve equal access and opportunity. Looking no further than your administration's *Blueprint* (U.S. Department of Education, 2010), a primary purpose of public education is to make sure that every student graduates from high school ready for college and a career. To use a legal term, asked and answered.

"From grade school on, we are all encouraged to cross the threshold of the classroom believing we are entering a democratic space—a free zone where the desire to study and learn makes us all equal" (hooks, 1994, p. 177). The democratic space that is mentioned here appears to have undergone significant modification during the 10 years that I was in the classroom, and much of that modification stems from the implementation of federal education policy. Looking no further than the reliance of your administration's *Blueprint* on data procured from standardized assessments, it is possible to bring to light the manner in which the implementation of this type of policy modifies classroom practice.

In the course of my recent experience as an urban school classroom teacher in Southern California, it was not an "all-of-a-sudden" type of phenomenon when the standards-based assessments were implemented, yet the insistence that these assessments were more important than other assessments sure seemed that way. Report cards were changed to more "accurately" reflect the "achievement" of students; no longer would letter grades be used but categories that directly corresponded to the description of a student's achievement level on standards-based assessments. Soon thereafter, changes to the typical school day resulted from this policy. Subjects such as language arts and math would become the preferred subjects of instruction because other subjects would not be tested on these standards-based assessments.

Federal policy emphasizes some subjects in the curriculum over other subjects. This can be clearly seen in the standardized testing of elementary school-age children in language arts and math but not in social studies or science (science testing does take place in fifth grade). I suppose it is possible to suggest that the subjects of language arts and math provide a broader foundation for the curriculum than social studies or science, but does that then mean that only language arts and math should be taught? Apple (2006) offers that the way this assumption implies what counts as legitimate knowledge is only that found on standardized assessments flies in the face of decades of contestation over the politics of knowledge and the inclusion of the languages, histories, and values of a country made of people and cultures from all over the world.

In schools where there are more community resources, this phenomenon is far less likely to occur. By community resources I'm not just talking about more money or parents who can volunteer before, during, and after school; I'm talking about parents who make a combined income above their respective state average, parents who live in the community and own their home, parents who are college educated. These parents are resources for their community in a way that is favorable to their local public school. Their daughters and sons are afforded the music lessons and the neighborhood sports teams, so if programs for music or physical education are cut from their public school, it's okay because they're getting them someplace else.

It is easy to misconstrue these contributions as "symbols" of caring. Those parents with resources to supplement their children's education can be perceived as "caring more" about their children or "valuing" education more than other parents. However, for those parents who do not possess those kinds of resources, there is often a form of condescension that accompanies this view of their economic disequilibrium. The thing is, these parents do care.

Changes to the curriculum had a substantial impact on a typical school day where I worked, and it wasn't long before the school culture began to change as a result. The administration at the school where I worked began to monitor to ensure that the bulk of instructional minutes were dedicated to language arts and math. Subjects like social studies, science, physical education, art, and music were marginalized and eventually discouraged. One of the surer ways to attract unwanted attention was to generate lesson plans that provided anything more than 20 minutes a day to any one of those subjects, and the audacity to attempt to teach all of them was frowned on. Again, the prerogative here was to increase test scores, and the consensus was that the best way to do this was to focus on teaching language arts and math.

There is an assumption that if test scores increase, then children are learning, teachers are teaching, parents are parenting, education has improved, and the public need is being met. This assumption gives the impression of being both logical and straightforward; maybe these scores and the accompanying assumptions are even indisputable evidence of a policy well crafted and aptly implemented. I would offer that an increase in test scores often does not indicate that education has improved, but that it simply means that scores have increased. The focus on high-stakes testing has narrowed the curriculum, and as schools face pressure to raise scores in reading and math, time has been reduced for learning other subjects or developing other knowledge. Teachers are forced to teach the test (Kumashiro, 2008).

Most of the students who I worked with were acquiring English as a second language, so it was not uncommon to have a wide range of fluency in the room. A typical classroom size was always more than 30 students, and with the exception of an instructional assistant for about an hour a day, it was just me with those students. Valuing their primary language was critical to engaging them and to their acquiring of a secondary language, as was taking the necessary time to support and discuss complex concepts and ideas. As I mentioned before, the school culture began to change, and one of the more dramatic shifts came with how we as a staff considered the placement of students in classes with less fluency.

As much as some would like to assume that the standardized scores so relied on to determine who is failing and who is not are indicators of improvement and progress for public education in the United States, there is evidence to the contrary. As much as some would like to assume that these scores purport to measure whether a school is progressing adequately, there is evidence to the contrary. "Policies that were put in place to raise standards, to increase test scores, to guarantee public accountability, and to make schools more competitive had results that were more than a little damaging to those students who were already the least advantaged in these same schools" (Apple, 2006, p. 77).

Due to the intense scrutiny that accompanied the label of "Program Improvement" and the pressure to increase scores at all costs, the school culture shifted to something less professional and probably less humane. Students with less fluency in English were regarded as liabilities to a classroom due to the likelihood that they would not perform as well on the standardized tests (all in English, of course) and would then "bring down" the overall performance of the class. With teachers now being evaluated by how their students performed on those standardized tests, the placement of students in classes became an outright pitched battle, with teachers attempting to influence and manipulate the makeup of their respective classes so that they were filled with students who had been identified as having a stronger fluency in English.

A few teachers went so far as to attempt to segregate the few students per grade level at the school who were "English only" (these are students whose primary language is English) into only one classroom, thus creating an "elite" class of students who were valued over others due to the fact that they would likely score higher on the standardized tests that had become so central to our collective functioning. This shift in culture quickly mutated, and it was not long before students who scored higher on the standardized tests were prized over all others by many teachers because of the way their performance would bolster the test scores of the class (again, teachers had begun to be evaluated by both the district and site administration based on these scores). This type of callous maneuvering was cancerous, spreading throughout the staff over several years, eventually leading to the kind of desperation one might expect to find during a shipwreck.

To be a successful professional educator, you have to care about your students, and it is this caring that is an integral part of both their learning and your own. This type of caring takes time because there needs to be trust between the students and teacher. For some trust comes quickly, and for others it comes more slowly; there is no standard formula. The last major effect on the school culture was how students were eventually perceived by the majority of the staff. Teachers began to care about students similar to the way that one cares about commodities; it's great when there is a high yield and not so great when the yield is low. I can vividly recall having a conversation with another teacher on staff who referred to her students who had not scored well on the previous year's test as "academic roadkill," and I knew that those students and many more like them were being approached, cared for, and taught with much the same attitude. The students understood this as well, and the intensity of this social dynamic simply increased every year.

Unintended Consequences

Often policy is affected by those closest to its crafting, those often referred to as policymakers, politicians, or "public servants." More often than not, these people have no experience in the field of education and yet consider their assumptions "expert opinion." It's perplexing to me because the people who should be affecting the education policy (professional educators) are typically the ones most segregated from the process. Those professional educators include, but are not limited to, teachers and university faculty, school nurses and librarians, site administrators, and district superintendents. Like any profession, there are varying degrees of education and experience and varying areas of expertise, so given the area in need, it would likely be necessary to narrow the focus to those most knowledgeable to that area of specialization in question. Why is it then when it comes to the policy regarding teaching as it pertains to public education that professional educators are largely ignored in favor of general assumptions? "Teacher-proofing education is an insult to teachers, as it assumes they are stupid and forces them to act as if they were stupid. It denies their will and creativity in the service of putting order into a system that often borders on the chaotic" (Kohl, 2003, p. 24). An analogy would be like having the American Bar Association regulated by people who had at some time an experience with the legal system, be it a parking ticket or because their brother-in-law is a police officer, or even because they've dialed 911 before. Obviously, this analogy overstates the point, but it does so because the exclusion of professional educators from policy is so understated, especially by those policy-makers who are in a position to invite and include them.

There often appears to be an abundance of reasoning found in the crafting of policy. Many of these "reasons" have little evidence to support them and are thus rightly considered assumptions. For example, let's take the assumption that teachers are not qualified to teach or if they are certified, that they are teaching well enough. Your *Blueprint* talks about this quite a bit. Notwithstanding the lack of a consensus of what "excellence" is, as it pertains to public education, the implication here is that there has not been enough recognition for teachers of excellence. Your suggestion of a new system of teacher evaluation to facilitate the increased recognition of excellence is predicated on the notion that standardized student assessment results are reliable data and provide authoritative evidence of student learning.

Clearly the desire to study and learn is becoming a value that is encouraged for some and discouraged for others even if the policy explicitly states otherwise. In my experience, I've seen the conditions that kids must endure: the overcrowding, the classrooms in trailers right next to a major six-lane street, and the unavailability of resources like access to a school library (because there was no money in the school budget to allocate for a librarian, but there was for a "resource teacher" whose sole function was to identify "underachieving students" for testing purposes). These conditions do not exist in those schools where the democratic space is still available, but that space has become the privilege of the few at the expense of the many.

Is this an unintended consequence of not caring? Does the policy, value those with means more than those without? I am not going to make a value judgment by suggesting that kids coming from neighborhoods that are on the lower end of socioeconomic status are somehow more deserving of these other subjects in the curriculum. It appears that the value judgment is already being made by the federal government's current educational policy and that judgment ignores the social conditions in which those children are immersed.

The emphasis placed by current policy on performing for these standardized assessments affects the practice of teaching in ways likely never considered (or *assumed*). So when the entire system of public education is set up as a meritocracy (as it is today) with winners and losers, what children are really learning is that they will either be a winner or a loser. So imagine, if you will, being mandated on a daily basis to attend an institution where you are constantly notified that you are a loser because you are not proficient in a particular subject, and due to this "deficiency" you will not be going to college and will not obtain employment that will allow you to make a living so that you may pursue your happiness. Pretty dreadful, right?

Advocating for a more democratic approach to education today can be futile in the standards-based assessment school culture. Equal opportunity is often no longer attempted, much less strived for; it can quite literally be every person for themselves—the students, the teachers, and the administrators. Cooperation has become a subjugated value, and being competitive— scoring the highest on a standardized test—became the measure of all education at the school. Finally, caring became a nostalgic afterthought that only a few remembered, valued, and practiced.

> We are children only once; and, after those few years are gone, there is no second chance to make amends. In this respect, the consequences of unequal education have a terrible finality. Those who are denied cannot be "made whole" by a later act of government. Those who get the unfair edge cannot be later stripped of what they've won. Skills, once attained—no matter how unfairly—take on a compelling aura. Effectiveness seems irrefutable, no matter how acquired. The winners in this race *feel* meritorious. Since they also are, in large part, those who govern the discussion of this issue, they are not disposed to cast a cloud upon the means of their ascent. (Kozol, 1991, p. 180)

The thing about competition is that there is always a winner and always a loser. It's great to be a winner in such a system but not so great to be the loser. Again, what is an unintended consequence of not caring? The message is clear: Win at all costs, otherwise no one will give a damn.

Lizbeth's Story

Being a teacher means that you are both a gatherer, and a teller, of stories. These stories cannot be expressed in numerical data and are widely considered irrelevant by some policymakers in relation to measuring whether the yearly progress of a school was adequately met. Of course, some of those same policymakers would likely counter with a statement about the inefficiency of storytelling and its irrelevance to more serious matters, such as being globally competitive. It is unfortunate that this is so because there is a significant amount of data and evidence found in stories.

I first met Lizbeth nearly 10 years ago at the outset of the beginning of her fourth-grade year and my second year of teaching full time at a public school. We had the opportunity to "loop" together as a class, and I remained the teacher for that same class for the fifth-grade year as well. I used to often remark to Lizbeth that she should think about becoming a lawyer—she was smart and outspoken, had a keen sense of what was fair and what was not, and did not hesitate to express her opinion, especially when she deduced that there was a need to be heard. I appreciated that about her then and do so to this day.

Lizbeth did well academically and socially both years we were together. She turned in her homework, participated in class, worked cooperatively when called on to do so, completed assignments to the best of her ability, and scored well on her standardized assessments. It seemed to me that she had a very bright future ahead of her and that she had the ambition to reach the goals that she had begun to design for herself. I still believe that about her—that she is both willing and able, intelligent and diligent, sincere and decent.

After fifth grade, Lizbeth left elementary school and attended the local middle school whose attendance boundary she resided within; same school district, same city. The middle school served students in sixth through eighth grades. Lizbeth walked to school every day, a little more than a mile each way from where she lived. She started sixth grade with great enthusiasm, attended honors classes, was a proud member of the Advancement via Individual Determination group ([AVID] a class comprised of students who were committed to attending college), and generally attended to her schooling the way that a young person does when they understand the value that it can hold for their future. Lizbeth's first year in middle school generally went well.

Lizbeth began her seventh grade year largely picking up where she had left off: She attended honors class and was again a member of AVID. It was also during this year that Lizbeth began to experience some of the less academic facets of the school culture. During that time, she became the target of bullying from another female student at the school. The details of the bullying can aptly be described as juvenile and culminated in a physical confrontation after school when the bully had followed Lizbeth on her way home. While the details of this event are juvenile, Lizbeth's handling of the occurrence was mature. She appealed first to a school official, her academic counselor (one of three counselors on staff at a school who served about 1,200 students, or one counselor for every 400 students), and the counselor advised that Lizbeth should just "ignore" the bully. Lizbeth had attempted to do just that prior to the altercation.

Lizbeth and her mom then appealed to the principal of the middle school. After a short meeting, the principal determined that the bullying *never actually happened* and that both Lizbeth and her mother were mistaken. No further explanation was provided to either Lizbeth or her mother. Exposed to the reality of this culture, she found herself without either refuge or recourse and endured two additional experiences of being bullied. Lizbeth conveyed to me that she was angry that the institutional guardians of the school were powerless, apathetic, or a combination thereof, to initiate and sustain any sort of meaningful change that would make the school that she attended less hostile.

In addition to the bullying, Lizbeth also had to withstand the misfortune of being placed in a class that was not intellectually aligned to her achievement. Although she continued to score well on standardized assessments and receive high marks from her teachers, she was mistakenly placed into a "low" language arts class during her eighth-grade year. Keenly aware that this placement would affect her opportunity to be placed in a honors class for her freshman year of high school (without prior placement in an honors class, it is virtually impossible for a student to be placed in an honors class the following year), Lizbeth once again appealed to her school counselor for a remedy. The school counselor refused to shift Lizbeth to another class, and it was not until Lizbeth's AVID teacher intervened that Lizbeth was transferred to the honors class.

Lizbeth was again subjected to bullying, and it was after that incident that her mom made the decision to move to another part of the city so that she could attend a different middle school. Lizbeth, her mom, and her younger sister and brother all moved during the winter break to another residence in the city so that Lizbeth could continue to pursue her education and her goal of attending college. Although Lizbeth was able to enroll and attend the new middle school (again, same city and same school district), she was placed in general education classes, not honors, due to the lack of resources of that middle school. She was able to finish her eighth-grade year without another incident of bullying. Despite of these unfortunate experiences, Lizbeth remained optimistic about attending high school.

During the summer that preceded Lizbeth's first year of high school, her aunt was diagnosed with cancer. Lizbeth's aunt lived in a neighboring city and was in need of care and assistance as she confronted this illness. Lizbeth insisted on caring for her aunt and agreed to move to her aunt's house to help care for her. Lizbeth knew that this meant transferring to a different school and a different school district.

Due to the logistics involved with the move (and outside her control), Lizbeth was enrolled into the new high school a week after school had started. Because of this delay, she was unable to enroll in the classes that she wanted to take. In addition, because this was a new school and a new school district, her prior academic achievements did not provide her with enough "status" to enroll in advanced classes. Lizbeth met with her guidance counselor and was informed that she would have to take what she got. Lizbeth appealed further to another guidance counselor and was informed that, although she made a compelling case for being placed in advanced classes, the administrative procedures needed to be followed, and, as such, only her assigned counselor could place her in those classes.

Completely on her own in the new school, Lizbeth attended to her studies with the same kind of dedication and care that she did while in middle and elementary school. She made repeated attempts to join the AVID class at the high school but was turned away. She attempted to join student government but was unable to mostly due to the highly competitive network that encapsulated such a competitive extra-curricular activity, one that shunned newcomers like Lizbeth. Still not discouraged, Lizbeth was able to participate in a program designed to inspire and prepare young people to attend college, facilitated by the city government where the high school was located.

Lizbeth completed her first 2 years of high school without incident. During that time, Lizbeth's aunt made a full recovery, and Lizbeth was able to move back with her mom. Rather than endure another transfer to another high school, the decision was made to keep her at her current high school and commute daily there. On days when her mom was not at work, she would make the half-hour to an hour drive to take Lizbeth to school. On days when her mom was at work, Lizbeth would take public transportation (the bus) to school. Either way, she always took the bus home from school.

The next 2 years of high school for Lizbeth provided her with typical challenges a young person encounters in high school, with one notable exception. Lizbeth was never counseled by anyone, either teacher or administrator, about college. Although she was a part of that extra-curricular program I mentioned earlier, the integration of that program with school officials was minimal and did not provide the type of culture that in-school programs (like AVID or honors classes) provided. During her third year, a critical year for those with interest in attending college, Lizbeth was never called in by her guidance counselor to discuss college, much less her future. When she was called in during the fall semester of her final year of high school, the counselor informed her that it was too late for her to apply to a four-year college and that she would just have to attend a local community college. Undaunted, Lizbeth made several attempts to position herself so that she could apply to other schools, including registering for and taking the SAT exam entirely on her own. However, she was unsuccessful with those attempts.

I am able to share this story now because Lizbeth has made it a point to keep in contact with me over the years. She recently invited me to her high school graduation, and I was afforded the opportunity to see her receive a high school diploma. It was a magnificent sight to behold, and I have no doubt that it was an honor to be present at such an occasion. Lizbeth and I have had many discussions since her graduation, and she affirms that despite her substantial efforts she fell short of her goal. I shared with her my disappointment too, and that I believed that the system had failed her as much as anything else. I also made it a point to communicate to her that in my opinion her efforts were valiant. So much of what she experienced was beyond her control. Imagine what could be if there were a policy that cared about her.

"The Realm of Control"

As a classroom teacher, certain things were within my realm of control and other things were not. For example, I was able to exert a significant amount of influence so as to provide a classroom environment that was conducive to learning. I did this by establishing classroom norms, constructing levels of expectations with regard to the curriculum and its mastery, and providing support to the individual learners in the room as well as the class as a whole. This structure that I created was an extension of my caring for all of the students in the class. My interaction with Lizbeth, for example, was contingent on my caring for her as much as it was that I wanted her to be "success-ful."

I was even able to withstand, at least partially, the assumption that the purpose of school was to become more highly competitive, not just with one's peers but also with other children of the world. This assumption is offered in your administration's *Blueprint*. When did being globally competitive become a decided goal of public education, perhaps even the whole point of going to school? I certainly didn't agree to that, and I know quite a few people who also didn't agree to that either.

> Admittedly, the economic needs of a society are bound to reflect to some rational degree within the policies and purposes of public schools. But, even so, most of us are inclined to ask, there must be something more to life as it is lived by six-year-olds or ten-year-olds, or by teenagers for that matter, than concerns about "success-ful global competition." Childhood is not merely basic training for utilitarian adult-hood. It should have some claims upon our mercy, not for its future value to the economic interests of competitive societies but for its present value as a perishable piece of life itself. (Kozol, 2005, pp. 94–95)

Public education as a platform for producing "globally competitive" citizens sounds to me more like a unilateral and arbitrary sound bite from a policymaker than it does an expressed need from a parent, a child, or an educator.

Public education in many communities has been transformed into a culture of merit, a culture of competition, and also a culture of survival. Macedo and colleagues (2003) remark that schools reproduce what is perceived as legitimate knowledge and make use of their institutional power to either affirm or deny a learner's lived experiences and culture. Withstanding the assumption (an assumption unintended surely but still one constructed from the application of federal policy) that the school's institutional power legitimated the knowledge of some of the children while illegitimating the knowledge of other children in our class was for me, at best, a delicate tightrope walk and, at worst, an evening spent reflecting whether I had done more harm than good. What I have observed is that for many children the data that result from standardized assessments are not being used as marks of progress but rather as badges of shame. Placing pressure on students to constantly demonstrate increased scores on standardized assessments, regardless of the level of support they may (or may not) receive from the school, irrespective of the impoverished conditions that may exist in the local communities and then to publicly display these results is a process of shaming (Apple, 2006).

These scores are being used to identify and label a child as "inferior" or "below basic." These scores chip away at the developing identity of a young person through an institutional process that would otherwise be considered an insult. Again, the balance between what was within my realm of control as a classroom teacher and what was outside the realm was fragile indeed. Although I might observe and record the progress of a student in the class, the data from the previous year's standardized assessment were being utilized by others to determine that the student was in need of further "support" from the school. This "support" typically took the form of a special meeting where the parents, the student, a school administrator, and myself all sat down to discuss the lack of proficiency in either language arts, math, or both as measured by the standardized assessment. These meetings began as early as second grade for students and would continue year in and year out until the student demonstrated a satisfactory level of proficiency on the assessment.

Within the realm of my control, I could privately reassure the parent that there was nothing wrong with their child and that he or she was making progress. I did this because I authentically cared about their child. However, the assumption that a young person is unaware of what is being implied is not the case; they are. Imagine being called into these special meetings year after year to hear roughly the same thing, namely, that you are not proficient, that you are "only" basic, below basic, or even far below basic. The inevitability of this kind of experience is completely predicated on the value (a value determined by current educational policy) placed on the data from these standardized assessments.

A lot of what a classroom teacher encounters when it comes to control is analogous to the experience of life as a whole. There are, quite simply, more things outside the realm of control of a classroom than within it. Circumstances outside this realm included just about everything else that occurs in a day of the life of a young person in the United States.

I could not control whether a child had a nutritious breakfast in the morning, and calling the free and/or reduced meal program at many public schools "nutritious" is yet another assumption that requires review. My caring was limited to what I could control, what was within "my realm." In commuting to and from school, Lizbeth may well have not had time to have breakfast, and the assumption that it was her fault or her mom's fault is inhumane and cruel given the circumstances with which she was working. I could not control whether a child would be able to safely navigate their neighborhood to and from school, and even Lizbeth's best efforts were thwarted by the institution that was responsible for her safety. Of course, with most of its resources devoted to increasing test scores, it is no small wonder why this occurred.

Finally, I could not control whether a child was able to carve out some time and space to work on concepts introduced during the school day; in short, there were far more things outside my realm of control than inside it. In caring for her aunt, Lizbeth had to find a balance between family and school, and in that process she determined what was valuable to her. The time and space she created for herself to work on school concepts, while still prioritizing the responsibility to her family, is commendable, and I admire her for the choices that she made. I would challenge anyone who begged to differ, who would suggest that because of those choices she made things "harder" on herself, that because of these choices she was positioned to be less competitive than others not faced with similar circumstances, and that because of these choices she had not done what was needed to continue her education and attend a university.

This chapter began with questions and has spent some time discussing simple and complex assumptions related to those questions. On any given day, one can walk into a classroom in a public school and observe teachers asking questions and students responding with possible answers, and vice versa. Good questions often don't have simple answers, and I think that recognizing this is valuable knowledge. One thing I learned very early on during my career as a classroom teacher was that I did not have all the answers, and often all I could respond with was, "That's a great question and I don't know the answer. What do you think? Maybe you can research that some more and get back to me with what you found and then we can share it with the class." I think that statement is apropos here as well.

Is it possible to legislate caring? What if we crafted a policy that expanded the realm that allowed more time and space for caring? What if that policy recognized that human experience is diverse, that the playing field is not level for everyone, and that there are times when people are forced to attend to circumstances that are beyond their control? Is it possible to craft such a policy, one that acknowledges both the value of achievement and the value of being human? If you asked Lizbeth, she'd say it is possible to expand the realm. I learned to listen to those young people I worked with like Lizbeth, to authentically consider their perspective as well as their story. I came to understand that my position in the world was in relation to their own, symbiotic and inclusive.

It is possible that this chapter is incomplete because it lacks a definitive answer. It is possible that an answer may become more definite after its consideration. It is possible to look forward, to strive, to resist with vigor forces that seek to oppress and dehumanize. It is possible to emphatically deny the standardization of experience and to insist that these actions be recognized. It is possible; it is possible.

References

Apple, M. (2006). *Educating the "right" way*. New York: Routledge.

hooks, b. (1994). *Teaching to transgress: Education as the practice of freedom*. NewYork: Routledge.

Kohl, H. (2003). *Stupidity and tears*. New York: The New Press.

Kozol, J. (1991). *Savage inequalities*. New York: Harper Perennial.

————. (2005). *The shame of the nation*. New York: Three Rivers Press.

Kumashiro, K. (2008). *The seduction of common sense*. New York: Teachers College Press.

Macedo, D., Dendrinos, B., & Gounari, P. (2003). *The hegemony of English*. Boulder, CO: Paradigm Publishers.

No Child Left Behind Act of 2001, 20 U.S.C.

U.S. Department of Education, Office of Planning, Evaluation and Policy Development, *ESEA Blueprint for Reform*. Washington, DC, 2010.

The Rights of Children: Policies to Best Serve 3-, 4-, and 5-Year-Olds in Public Schools[1]

Ben Mardell, Lisa Fiore,
Marina Boni, & Melissa Tonachel

Driven by concerns about future economic competitiveness and the need for a well-educated workforce, the education and care of American preschoolers are in the midst of a profound transformation. Increasing numbers of 3- and 4-year-olds are receiving a significant part of their education and care out of their homes. The potential of increased government funding raises the promise of improving the quality and availability of this education, vastly improving the lives of young children. At the same time, classroom practices illsuited for preschoolers raise the specter of a brave new world of early education that will do more harm than good, both to the immediate quality of children's experiences and the long-term impact of early education.

In this chapter, we focus on the most intriguing and problematic part of this transformation: the inclusion of 3- and 4-year-olds in public schools. For better or worse, public schools are poised to play a major role in American early education. As model programs are identified through the allocation of federal Race to the Top funds[2], and potentially Early Childhood challenge Grants[3], the next few years will be a pivotal in shaping policies regarding how young children are served in public schools. Our goal here is to identify policies that will ensure that the money supporting public school preschools is spent wisely in the best interests of children and society.

We begin by surveying the changing landscape of American early childhood education and then explain our concerns about preschool in public schools. These concerns are, in part, raised by the experience of kindergarten, whose shift away from a "children's garden" to a junior first grade raises red flags about the expansion of preschool in public schools. To safeguard against preschool suffering a similar fate, we identify three rights young children have in any classroom setting:

- the right to be recognized and listened to,
- the right to learn through play, and
- the right to meaningful, purposeful, and reasonable evaluation.

We then offer beacons of hope, three public school preschools where children's rights are respected and where there is joy in learning. We conclude by naming 10 policies regarding curriculum, assessment, personnel, and the organization of preschool in public schools. These policies include a requirement to allot 50% time to play, no testing of 4-year-olds, and creating robust early childhood departments (with purview over kindergarten as well as preschool).

Our focus should not be seen as an endorsement of public schools as the best venue for educating young children. In order to meet the needs of all families, we support a mixed delivery system that includes family day care, Head Start, corporate day care, and community-based child care centers. Indeed, we want to bring what is best from community child care—a respect for childhood and a responsiveness to children—into the public schools.

The Changing Landscape of American Early Education

Where and how American 3- and 4-year-olds spend their time has changed radically over the last half century. In 1960, it was unusual for these children to attend "school"; only 10% of 3- and 4-year-olds had any classroom experience. With the advent of Head Start and an increase of mothers in the workforce, this figure doubled by 1970. By 1990, 40% of 3- and 4-year-olds were attending some type of preschool. Five years later, when Georgia established the first statewide universal pre-kindergarten program, half of all 3- and 4-year-olds received some type of out-of-home education (Barnett, Robin, Hustedt, & Schulman, 2003). Today 35% attend some type of center-based preschool, 22% take part in Head Start, and 22% of 4-year-olds are enrolled in public preschools. Only 26% of 4-year-olds receive no out-of-home education and care (Barnett, Hustedt, Friedman, Boyd, & Ainsworth, 2007).

Although parents continue to pay for the bulk of their children's preschool experiences, the last 50 years have also seen a significant increase in the amount of governmental support for early education and care. In 1970 (after the advent of Head Start), 70% of education and care for preschoolers took place in private programs. By 1995, that rate had decreased to 52%

(Barnett et al., 2003). Increasingly, public schools are opening government-funded preschool classrooms. In 2006, two thirds of the children attending publicly funded preschools were in public school programs (Wilson, 2008).

The economic, social, demographic, and political forces responsible for these changes are likely to continue and even accelerate. In the minds of an increasing number of Americans, preschool is now seen as an important part of a child's educational experiences, something that society should, at least in part, support (Chaudhuri & Potepan, 2009).

Emblematic of this shift is a report released in late 2009 titled "Military Leaders for Kids, Ready, Willing and Unable to Serve." Co-signed by more than 80 retired military leaders, including former chiefs of staffs Generals John Shalikashvili and Henry Shelton, the report argues that, "Investing in our children through early education is not a Republican issue or Democratic issue. It's a plain common sense issue critical to our National Security....National Security in the year 2030 is absolutely dependent on what's going on in pre-kindergarten today." The military leaders conclude, "A top national and state priority must be to increase the number of children served by early education...and it is equally important to deliver high quality programs" (Mission Readiness, 2009).

Echoing arguments and citing studies common in other reports advocating for expanding government support for early education, this report lays out an urgent problem. For the generals, the problem is a lack of eligible recruits for the military; in most other reports, it is the need for a skilled workforce to compete in the global economy. Regardless of how the problem is defined, the case for how increased funding for early childhood will redress it tends to begin with the headline that the "most important changes" in brain development occur during the first 5 years of life. Longitudinal research on the effects of early childhood education is cited next. The iconic High/Scope Perry Preschool Program from Ypsilanti, Michigan, along with more recent studies, provides evidence that preschool increases high school graduation rates and lowers incarceration rates (Barnett & Masse, 2007; Schweinhart, Barnes, & Weikart, 1993). These findings are the basis of cost-benefit analyses that conclude there are "solid savings to taxpayers" to investing in early childhood education.

This is a compelling narrative. It has been presented by early childhood advocates for decades (although without the "hard science" of brain research). What is new and significant is that the argument for public support for early childhood education is now being made by military and business leaders, economists, and a host of well-financed nonprofit organizations (Fuller, 2007). This narrative is embraced by politicians and the general public. Republican governors and a Democratic president support universal pre-kindergarten.

The results are impressive. Thirty-seven states now financially support 4-year-olds attending school. Following an intensive lobbying effort by early childhood advocates, the federal Department of Education opened the Race to the Top fund to pre-kindergarten programs (Young, 2009). Despite the Great Recession's devastating impact on state budgets, universal pre-kindergarten has fared relatively well especially when compared with other social programs (Pew Center on the States, 2010). It seems likely that an improved economy will see the continuation of the trend towards increased funding for early childhood education.

This has the potential to be very good news. Money has been the longstanding barrier to quality early childhood education for all. Advocate Gwen Morgan's term "the child care trilemma" captures the issue—a zero-sum game pitting the interests of teachers, families, and the quality of care against one another. Consider one part of the trilemma, teacher compensation. The salaries of preschool teachers are shamefully low. The average preschool teacher makes $24,000, compared with $59,000 for elementary school teachers and $21,000 for parking lot attendants (Bureau of Labor Statistics, 2006; Salary.com, 2010). The results are not surprising: high turnover rates (17% a year) and a lack of training and credentials for many teachers (Herzenberg, Price, & Bradley, 2005). Historically, increasing salaries would have to be paid for by parents in the form of higher tuitions or taken from the other resources that are needed to provide children with quality experiences—crayons, blocks, healthy snacks, and the like. Neither option held much appeal. Families were already spending 10% or more of their income on child care. Centers, many operating out of church basements, had little fat to trim from the nonpersonnel parts of their budgets.

Public support provides a way out of the child care trilemma. Teachers' salaries can be increased without hurting families or the quality of care. In fact, increasing salaries improves the quality of care. As the principles of labor economics explain, higher salaries mean better retention rates and, over time, a larger and more qualified pool of potential teachers. A living wage for early childhood educators (pre-kindergarten teachers working in the Boston

Public Schools can earn upward of $80,000 a year) will lead to a greater pro-fessionalization of the field with clear benefits to children and their families. Thanks to the tireless efforts of thousands of advocates, for the first time in our county's history, there is the possibility of high-quality education and care for all 3- and 4-year-olds.

So Why the Worry?

How could the possibility of billions of dollars in new funding for early childhood education be anything other than a cause for great celebration? How could parents receiving free preschool and teachers earning a decent wage be anything other than a good thing? Simply put, we worry that the context of public schools will create pressures to push practices down from elementary grades that are inappropriate for and even harmful to young children.

Our concerns are grounded in observations (our work takes us to scores of schools) and an analysis of the larger context of American education. We have seen public school classrooms where 4-year-olds are spending far too much time sitting and being talked to by adults and far too little time engaged in active exploration of materials and in play. In too many classrooms, the block area has disappeared, and, beyond pencils and markers (intended to practice writing), art supplies are minimal. We have seen classrooms where families are barred from entering and where 4-year-olds are not allowed to sit on teachers' laps.

To understand how things could go so wrong, it is necessary to consider education in America today, where the dominant narrative is that of the ac-countability movement. The premise of the accountability movement is that American public schools are (or were) failing, particularly for African American, Hispanic, and low-income children. The solution is found in high standards (for children, teachers, and administrators) and accountability based on tests in core academic subjects. Codified into national policy in the No Child Left Behind (NCLB) legislation, every public school in American is required to make Adequate Yearly Progress on state tests.

These tests are the coin of the realm. Based on test scores, schools can be sanctioned or even closed, children uprooted, jobs lost, and mayoral elections decided. Reputations of principals, superintendents, and state commissioners of education are determined, in large measure, by test scores.

At the same time, the key leaders of public schools are generally not early childhood educators. Most have neither significant training in child development nor a strong understanding of preschool curriculum. Their image of a classroom comes from their familiarity with elementary or high schools. The result is that pedagogical practices from elementary school are pushed down into preschool. Although the state accountability tests do not officially start until third grade, their influence is felt throughout public schools. It is not uncommon to hear a first-grade teacher justify a practice on the grounds of "getting them ready for the test." It is fair to say that preparation for the tests begins the day a child enters school.

What is appropriate preparation? Those not familiar with child development are too often tempted to make preschool simply a junior version of kindergarten and first grade, with a narrow focus on skills that map directly onto the tests. The problem is that much that is important and valuable about preschool is discarded in the process. Going faster does not mean going farther. At age 4, preparation for school should focus on learning how to learn, how to solve problems, how to focus, and how to tell a story. It should foster curiosity, excitement, and engagement in the learning process. It should involve learning to self-regulate and defer gratification. It should not involve worksheets or drills for skills that children will appropriately develop as they proceed in school.

There is also the problem of personnel. Because the tests do not begin until third grade, upper elementary grades can be viewed as more important (at least to the immediate career prospects of administrators and the reputation of schools and districts). Preschool can become the dumping grounds where principals put their weakest teachers, teachers who may be woefully unprepared to work with 4-year-olds. For new teachers, regulations for the licensing require a shorter period of training with mentor teachers in preschool or kindergarten and more time working in first or second grade, focusing attention on skills appropriate for older children.

We wish our concerns were a misreading of the American educational landscape. We are convinced they are not, and we invite those who disagree to consider what has happened to kindergarten in America.

The Cautionary Tale of Kindergarten

When Friedrich Froebel developed his ideas about kindergarten (German for "children's garden") in the 1800s, the notion of designing education for young children was revolutionary. Froebel's kindergarten challenged traditional beliefs, introducing concepts such as children learning through play, developmental appropriateness, and connecting children and their learning to nature. The focus was on the whole child rather than on a narrow band of academic skills.

Teachers were trained in kindergarten education so that they could be effective guides for children's thinking, rather than solely transmitters of information. In this capacity, teachers also engaged families in their children's educational process. Using close observation of children as the main source of data, Froebel argued that teachers could assess children's learning. He also stressed the value of listening to children through informal interviews and documentation, thereby validating their ideas and understandings.

The original American kindergartens were private enterprises, separate from schools for older children. At the beginning of the 20th century, kindergartens started to be added to public schools, although often as part-time programs. Slowly, states began mandating that kindergartens be part of public schools; in 2009 New Hampshire became the last state to require school districts to provide kindergarten (Benson, 2008). Over time the length of the kindergarten day has also increased, an initiative that has gained momentum as the importance of early education has been recognized. The resulting economic calculus has led to a migration of families and teachers to public kindergartens. Today there are few independent, private kindergartens, and the number of programs for 5-year-olds that were previously part of child care centers has been significantly reduced. Only 2% of all kindergartners attend private, nonsectarian schools—a figure that includes classrooms that are part of elementary schools (National Center for Education Statistics, 2009).

The image that kindergarten still evokes for many is of a children's garden, complete with stories, snacks, singing, dramatic play, craft projects, nature walks, and a class pet. The accountability movement is making this image increasingly obsolete. The kindergarten of old has been swept away by the pressures to prepare children for standardized tests. Kindergarten is now the new first grade. Dramatic play and blocks have been replaced with prescribed curricula focused on reading, writing, and math. Children are tested regularly on their math and literacy skills.

The extent of these changes is shocking. A survey of 268 kindergartens in New York City and Los Angeles public schools found kindergartens in name only. Children in Los Angeles spend 88 minutes a day receiving literacy instruction, 47 minutes receiving math instruction, and 21 minutes being tested or receiving test prep. Blocks, sensory materials, and dramatic play are largely gone. Play has virtually disappeared. On average, only 19 minutes of the school day are allotted to child-initiated choices (including play) (Alliance for Childhood, 2009). Concerned kindergarten teachers rightfully label this situation dangerous and even "abusive." It certainly does not constitute a sound environment for young children's learning. As early childhood educator Winifred Hagan (cited in Hartigan, 2009) explains, "Kids are spending hours of their day sitting with pencils and tracing dotted lines. And we call that education? We are kidding ourselves."

Families with requisite financial and/or human resources have often shielded their children from these changes by sending them to private child care centers that do not suffer the pressures of mandatory testing and by delaying their transition to kindergarten. The impact of delayed entry into formal kindergarten has resulted in a shift in the demographics of preschool and kindergarten students. Forty years ago, 96% of 6-year-old children were enrolled in first grade or above. As of 2005, the figure was just 84%. School attendance for this age group has not changed. Rather, more and more 6-year-olds are now in kindergarten. Only a quarter of this change can be attributed to changes in school district age requirements. Most is the result of "academic red-shirting," parents keeping children out of school until they are older (Deming & Dynarski, 2008). Research confirms the wisdom of red-shirting, finding academic benefits to delaying entry into school. But red-shirting comes with significant economic costs to families in the form of child care and deferred income (West, Meek, & Hurst, 2000). White males are twice as likely to be red-shirted as their African American counterparts, and it is reasonable to assume that affluent families are better able to absorb the economic costs of keeping children out of school than poor families. The transformation of kindergarten may very well be accentuating the achievement gap.

The Rights of Children in Classroom Settings

Four-year-olds do not vote. They do not send emails to their representatives. Only when they are brought along by parents do they attend protest rallies. In summary, they do not constitute a powerful interest group that can advocate for their rights. This does not mean that they do not have rights. Four-year-olds are citizens, not potential citizens, not citizens in training, but citizens, with rights and obligations like all citizens.

The rights of children go beyond the pedagogical rights we name here (see the Convention on the Rights of the Child, adopted by the UN General Assembly in 1989). Children have the right to adequate nutrition, safe homes and neighborhoods, and access to medical care. They have the right to life, liberty, and the pursuit of happiness. All children have these rights. But the nature of these rights, and how they are manifested in school, depends on children's ages. Four-year-olds are very different from fourth graders. They have different brains. They have different bodies. They have different relationships with their families. They have different social and emotional needs. They have different interests. They learn in different ways. It is not that they have difficulty paying attention (as is sometimes said of them). Rather, because of their developing brains, they cannot help paying attention to everything that is going on around them.

Preschoolers need to move, to touch, to talk, and to play in order to learn. It is against their nature to walk silently in a line down a hallway. Although they can be trained to sit quietly, during a phonemic awareness lesson it is just as likely that they will be studying the pattern on the rug as attending to the teacher.

Here we focus on three rights young children have in classroom settings, rights that support their pursuit of happiness and the development of their long-term potential.

The Right to Be Recognized and Listened to

To know and support a child as a learner, teachers must pay very careful attention to the choices she makes, to the language she uses, to her interactions, and to the themes she revisits. Children must be recognized not just as growing, unfinished beings, but as true thinkers and doers, as active participants in their education. Each child comes to a classroom setting as a member of a family and cultural group(s) with specific language and practices; she comes with a particular worldview shaped by her experiences, which in turn shapes her actions, ideas, and interactions. The UN Convention recognizes the views of the child as distinct and legitimate and specifically names the child's right to express those views (Articles 12–14). With the child's right to expression comes adults' responsibility to listen.

Not only do children have a right to be listened to, but paying close attention to children fosters their learning. The role of the teacher is critical in forming relationships with children and structures in classrooms that facilitate listening and signal recognition. The teaching of academic skills and concepts is supported by teaching in a responsive, intellectually rigorous environment. Carlina Rinaldi (2001) writes, "Listening is the basis for any learning relationship. Through action and reflection, learning takes shape in the mind of the subject, and through representation and exchange, becomes knowledge and skill." Following the training of teachers in Scandinavia with practices focused on listening, children were found to be more confident in sharing their views and opinions and would listen for longer periods of time to teachers and peers. Children who previously were reluctant to talk in groups were more confident about doing so (Kinney, 2005).

The right to be listened to may seem obvious (as rights are often self-evident), but it is far from guaranteed. It may seem there is no time in the school day to embark on an exploration of child-driven topics because there is other material teachers are mandated to cover.

In the end, we want children to be engaged, communicative, and invested in their learning. But, as Sergio Spaggiari, a director of the Reggio Emilia municipal preschools, observes, "When children feel they are not being listened to, they don't have anything to say." If our responsibilities include bringing our youngest citizens more fully into participation in our communities, then listening is a sure beginning.

The Right to Learn Through Play

Play is a core resource of childhood (Carlsson-Paige, 2008). Play is more than fun (which is a good in and of itself); play is how children learn. Play helps the young brain develop. Especially in urban settings where many young children struggle with past or ongoing trauma, play is the medium through which they resolve the upsets that can otherwise make them unavailable to learn in school.

Among the numerous social, emotional, and intellectual skills and dispositions that are enhanced through play, we focus on three that are essential for children to succeed in school and participate in the 21st-century economy: self-regulation, symbolic thinking, and collaboration.

Self-regulation, a child's ability to monitor her actions and control her impulses, is critical to school success. In first grade and beyond, children are required to be self-directed and independent learners. They need to wait, follow directions, and manage their time. They need to focus their attention, make plans, and persist in meeting goals. Play provides the perfect contexts for 3- and 4-year-olds to develop self-regulation (Bronson, 2000). In play, children have the opportunity to manage their own behavior. They have the chance to plan out actions and follow through on their ideas. They have the opportunity for sustained engagement in situations that are compelling to them.

Play is also an important context to develop symbolic thinking. The adult world is filled with symbols. Squiggles on a page can provide directions on how to prepare a meal, build a bridge, or play a sonata. The path to mastery over these symbol systems begins by understanding that one thing can represent something else. In play, children learn a piece of paper can be gold, a chair can be a rocket ship, and two toilet paper rolls can become binoculars. Here lies the foundation for success in literacy, math, and other symbol systems.

The science lab, the business group, the art ensemble—virtually all high-level work in our society involves collaboration, and play is the genesis of children being able to work together. When a child in the house area says to a friend, "I'm the Mommy, you're the baby," she is creating a collective plan. In play, children assign roles, make joint plans and follow through on them, and encounter and often solve the inevitable problems that social interactions involve. Through play, children learn how to accommodate their desires to the desires of others. They learn leadership and followership. Through play, children learn how to work together.

All children deserve the right to learn through play; it is not a luxury to be afforded only to the privileged. For children living in poverty, who may have less access to venues and props that promote quality play (e.g., safe playgrounds, open-ended toys), preschool can provide the exact kind of play environment they need to be prepared to succeed in school. As the National Association for the Education of Young Children (NAEYC) explains, "Because of how they spend their time outside of school, many young children now lack the ability to play at the high level of complexity and engagement that affords so many cognitive, social and emotional benefits. As a result, it is vital for early childhood settings to provide opportunities for sustained high-level play and for teachers to actively support children's progress towards such play" (Copple & Bredekamp, 2008). In play, every child becomes, in the words of Lev Vygotsky (1978), "above their age, above their daily behavior; in play, it is as though he was a head taller than himself."

The Right to Meaningful, Purposeful, and Reasonable Evaluation

A yearly trip to the doctor should be on every 4-year-old's calendar. However, for a healthy child, weekly exams would be intrusive and even abusive. The same is true for educational evaluation; some is reasonable, whereas too much violates children's rights.

There are three reasons for evaluation in preschool: (a) making sound decisions about teaching and learning, (b) identifying significant concerns that may require focused intervention for individual children, and (c) helping programs improve their educational practices (National Association for the Education of Young Children, 2003). To make sound decisions about teaching and learning, educators need to collect ongoing, formative assessment, information that captures not only the product but also the process of their students' learning. Teachers need to know about their charges' interests, understandings, and misunderstandings in order to plan the next steps in the learning process. Occasional summative assessment, guided by the Work Sampling System or other measures that collect data in the context of children's explorations of materials and play, can also be useful in identifying children's strengths and monitoring their progress in important domains. To identify and better understand concerns about specific children, teachers need to identify children who may have cognitive, social, or emotional difficulties and refer these individual children to specialists who can administer the appropriate test to evaluate the child's difficulty. To make program improvements and ensure early childhood funds are being spent wisely, whole classrooms should be evaluated using sound quality measures.

Yet as the number of tests to measure preschoolers have multiplied and as data-gathering and analytic technologies have grown more sophisticated and less expensive, the impulse to use the elementary school practice of testing individual children using standardized, norm-referenced instruments has grown. Although not legally required, some administrators may see testing of even young children as the way to ensure accountability. In some public school preschools, up to 6 weeks a year are devoted to testing.

Standardized tests to collect data on preschoolers' emerging literacy and math skills do little to improve children's lives. Teachers do not need tests to get the information they need to guide their instruction of 3- and 4-year-olds;

close observation of children provides far more useful data (Kohn, 2001). Further, testing preschoolers often produces misleading results. Young children cannot sit and concentrate for long on tasks that have little connection to their interests. They may not understand test questions, and their performance can be affected by anxiety, hunger, fatigue, and stress. Because of this, the odds that a test given to a preschooler or kindergartner will give accurate results are only 50% (Alliance for Childhood, 2009).

Moreover, testing comes at a cost. Teaching can be derailed by taking time away from the curriculum. A common refrain we hear from teachers is, "I haven't done much with the kids this week because I've been testing." Valerie Gumes, a principal in an early learning center that is part of a public school system, explains, "I'm not opposed to standards, but [to] the amount of time we spend doing these assessments. It's really criminal" (cited in Hartigan, 2009).

There are psychological costs as well. A colleague of ours reported administering a math assessment to a 5-year-old student, who at one point looked up at her and asked in a sorrowful tone, "I'm losing, aren't I?" Kohn (2001) reports of young children "bursting into tears or vomiting in terror, their incipient self-confidence dissolving along with their composure." This kind of testing must stop.

The bottom line is that pedagogical practices in preschools should be very different from those in elementary school classrooms. From what is on the walls, to the materials in the room, to the setup of furniture, to the schedule of the day, to the training of the teachers, preschool classrooms should be very different from their traditional counterparts in the elementary grades. It may even be a mistake to call them classrooms; "workshops" or "learning and play centers" may be better terms. As more and more public school preschools come online, the task is not to make children ready for schools but to make schools ready for children.

Three Beacons of Hope

This survey of kindergarten could lead to the conclusion that public schools are no place for 3- and 4-year-olds. We resist this conclusion in recognition of the necessity and appeal for many families of enrolling their children in public schools. The work of colleagues whose teaching respects and promotes the rights of preschoolers demonstrates the promise of preschool in public schools. Although examples could come from a host of dedicated educators from around the country, here we offer vignettes from three class-rooms in a large, urban public school system.

In her integrated classroom, Chris Bucco has gathered her 3- and 4-year-old students to listen to and enact Caitlin's story, loosely based on "Goldi-locks and the Three Bears." Chris narrates as Caitlin (Mama Bear), Zander (Papa Bear), and Mishka (Baby Bear) run away from Marina (Goldilocks). But after Goldilocks leaves the bears' house, she gets her due. She is bitten by William, who plays the dreaded no-see-ums of the New England woods. As the performance ends, the actors bow in response to applause from their classmates.

Chris is particularly pleased that Caitlin has become engaged in the sto-rytelling program. One of the 7 of Chris' 15 students identified with a disa-bility: Caitlin has been diagnosed with autism. This activity helps Caitlin learn how to engage in dramatic play, taking on roles and negotiating with peers. It also allows Chris to get to know this reserved child better. All the children enjoy the storytelling. The enactments create a sense of community where, in Chris' words, "Kids come together and really listen to each other." She adds, "If we could do this all the time, the kids and I would be in heav-en."

Jenny Frazier teaches 20 four-year-olds at a school 1 mile away from a major international airport. So it is not surprising that in reviewing her obser-vational notes, Jenny finds an intense interest in flight. This interest appears when Juan and Miguel build planes in the block area, when Maria makes kites in the art studio, when Pablo, Karen, and Gabriella fly off to Mexico in the dramatic play area, and when Peter excitedly talks about the birds he has just seen.

Jenny decides to create some curriculum on flight. She begins by asking her students what they know and what they wonder about. She learns that the children see birds, planes, and balloons as equivalent in their ability to fly, so she plans activities that will help children build richer understandings of flight. She invites some third graders to help the children construct paper air-planes. She provides photos of flying objects (eagles, airplanes) that the chil-dren refer to as they construct models in the art studio. She brings in a helium balloon to provoke a discussion about how (and if) balloons fly. She stocks the dramatic play area with props that evoke plane travel. And she plans a trip to the airport.

David Ramsey often asks his 3- and 4-year-old charges what they want to do during outside time. On one occasion, they decide they want to play baseball but then realize they need a bat. Kenya informs the group that "I have a bat at home," which might solve the problem, except for the fact that the bat is at her house. Jamie suggests, "Mr. David, you could drive us [to Kenya's house]." David wonders aloud if all the children could fit in his car. When it seems most of his students think this possible, he asks them how many people will have to be squeezed into his car. After a brief period of calling out ("10," "12," "14," "23," "a lot"), David suggests that whoever wants to could count, but that this should be done one at a time. Everyone takes a turn, and David recaps the results: "I noticed that there were two numbers I heard several times: 12 and 14. Is one of these numbers the right number of people here in the Yellow Room?" Some children call out that there are 12 children, but others remember there are also two teachers.

After the children agree that the adults (David and the assistant teacher) need to be included in order to drive, David proposes going outside to see whether the group can fit into his car. After a safety message, the group discovers that all 12 preschoolers can squish into a Toyota Camry. But then David raises the obvious problem: "What about me and Ms. Stevens?" Kenya suggests that the class should use Ms. Stevens' car, and David again asks about the adults. Kenya replies, "No, we can put four kids in your car and four kids in Ms. Stevens's car." Jamie notices, "But wait. That won't work! That's not all the kids. That's only eight." After some back and forth between the children, Daniel lands on "Six. We need six. Put six in your car and six in Ms. Stevens' car." Jamie agrees, "That's the way to do it. Then there won't be any kids left over." David again raises the issues of drivers, and Jamie modifies her answer: "You need to go in your car, and Ms. Stevens needs to go in her car. Then we have seven and seven."

Chris, Jenny, and David listen, create opportunities to learn through play, and use evaluation to support learning. Their work is supported by some of the policies of their school district, but it is also undercut by the pressures inherent in being part of a public school system. All three teachers bemoan the fact that they are not able to carry out the practices described above as often as they would like. To encourage and nurture more of such good teaching, to ensure that the promise of preschools is met in public school, we recommend the following policies regarding curriculum, assessment, personnel, and organization.

Policies to Protect the Rights of Children in Classroom Settings
Curriculum

Require 50% of school time for play. Play is fun—an avenue for preschoolers to pursue their right to happiness. But play is also more than fun; it is a primary means by which preschoolers learn. Because of its seemingly random and purposeless nature, play can be a hard sell in the current educational climate demanding rigor, accountability, and fidelity to standards. Preschool play can seem noisy, chaotic, and unproductive. Understanding the role of play in preschoolers' learning redefines play as meaningful engagement that fosters self-regulation, symbolic thinking, and collaboration.

It is critical to remember that the High/Scope Perry Preschool Program, along with other preschool programs that produce important, long-term gains, is play based. A comparison between High/Scope and programs devoid of play found children from the former to be better socially adjusted as they entered adulthood and a third less likely to have committed a serious crime (Schweinhart et al., 1993).

It takes a skilled teacher to facilitate play. The teacher's role begins with providing stimulating materials that connect with children's interests (as Jenny Frazier did in her flight curriculum). Teachers must also know when and how to support play, helping children who are not yet skilled at developing scenarios and negotiating the complex social dynamics of play. Teachers must be careful not to deprive children of the opportunity to direct their own play. Children cannot learn self-regulation unless they are allowed to regulate themselves.

Public school preschoolers must enjoy important literacy and math experiences, often best delivered through prescribed curricula. Yet there will always be pressure to add more specific content and skills to the curriculum. A second-grade teacher might complain that her new charges have poor handwriting and insinuate that children should begin formal instruction on letter formation in preschool. A new report may bemoan fourth graders' lack of basic geographical knowledge and recommend a curriculum beginning in preschool to help remedy the situation. These demands require time. To ensure that essential learning is taking place, 50% of school time must be reserved for play and active explorations.

Children's storytelling should play a major role in preschool curriculum. Like play, storytelling prepares children for the future by supporting their language and literacy development. Allyssa McCabe and her colleagues (2009) implemented a story dictation program in a preschool classroom where 75% of the students received free or reduced lunch and 40% were non-native English speakers. Compared with a control group, the children who told stories had significant gains in their receptive vocabulary and the quality of their oral narratives, the two most powerful predictors of fourth-, seventh-, and tenth-grade reading comprehension (Snow, Porche, Tabors, & Harris, 2007).

As Chris Bucco has discovered, stories are a central way that children pursue their happiness. Just as birds build nests and bees make honey, people tell stories. Stories are a central way that we communicate and organize our thoughts (Bruner, 1986). Stories are how children explain who they are and learn about each other. Stories help teachers to listen to their students.

Create structures to institutionalize responsiveness to children's interests. Public school districts run on published curricula. Fortunately, there are some prescribed curricula that are appropriate for young children. For example, Opening the World of Learning (OWL) is a book-rich program that pre-scribes almost 50% of its time to children's self-directed activities (Schekendanz & Dickenson, 2003). Yet even with the best-scripted curricula, flexibility is essential in order to create compelling, responsive learning experiences for young children. Teachers must have time and permission to pursue a study of flight or to see whether everyone in the class can fit into a Toyota Corolla.

In his recent book *Drive*, Daniel Pink (2009) tells of an Australian soft-ware company where once a month the programmers are told to work on anything they want. The only requirement is that at the end of the day they report on what they did. These "Do your own thing" days have become the company's most productive days. Published curricula can be useful guides for teachers, but in order to bring real excitement and passion into preschool classrooms, explicit structures must exist that allow teachers to follow their students' interests. One day a month, one day a week, or every afternoon should be set aside to allow children and teachers to pursue their interests. This is not time off but time to use proven practices that create compelling curricula, time to pursue projects and products valued by the children (see Katz & Chard, 1989; Project Zero & Reggio Children, 2001 for examples).

Assessment

Assessment that supports listening. The Greek root for assessment is "to sit beside." In order to follow children's interests, teachers need to listen carefully, to sit beside their students. Assessment should be used, as Jenny Frazier does, to plan compelling curriculum. Through anecdotal notes, photographs, and video, which she shares and analyzes with colleagues, Jenny collects data that help her identify her students' interests and their thinking strategies. She uses assessment to listen.

No testing 4-year-olds. It is important that we ensure that money for preschool is spent wisely: rich classrooms set up and run properly, sensitive teachers providing high-quality education. Accountability is necessary.

Accountability can be achieved by using quality rating systems such as the Early Childhood Environment Rating Scale (ECERS) (Harms, Clifford, & Cryer, 1998). The ECERS assesses the appropriateness of the classroom environment, child–teacher interactions, program structure, and the curriculum. It provides data to improve programs and identify failing ones. With such tools, there is no need to subject preschoolers to standardized tests. NAEYC also rates programs according to these and other criteria, including assessment and family communication, through its process of accreditation.

Personnel

Only preschool teachers should teach preschoolers. Facilitating play and creating responsive curricula are complex tasks. Those who teach preschoolers must have early childhood training. Just as it would be unreasonable to send a preschool teacher to middle school, it is folly to expect quality results when elementary teachers work with 4-year-olds. It is unacceptable for school districts to classify preschool as "junior kindergarten" and then assign a sixth-grade teacher who has a K-6 license to teach preschool. It will come as no surprise that Chris, Jenny, and David have their degrees in early childhood education.

In the same vein, to ensure that kindergartners receive the education they deserve, their teachers must have specific early childhood training. Policymakers must say no to including kindergarten in elementary teaching certificates. It is naïve to think that a teacher training program can adequately prepare teachers to effectively meet the broad changes that occur in children from ages 5 through 12. Kindergarten teachers must know how to support play, lead responsive curricula, and listen closely to young children. To do this, they need intensive early childhood training.

Mandatory training for administrators. Schools that house preschools need administrators with knowledge of preschoolers. The principals of schools with 4-year-olds should attend training geared to help them understand the unique requirements and needs of teaching young children. They need to know, for example, that young children need physical contact with adults and parents should be welcomed into preschool classrooms. They need to be encouraged to create and support policies and practices of preschool that will be very different than those for elementary grades.

Coaching to support teachers. Facilitating rich and dynamic play, providing responsive curricula, helping children become better storytellers, integrating children's interests, and supporting their skill development by following their interests (as David did in bringing math into the search for a baseball bat) is akin to rocket science: It is high-skilled work best done in a team. Preschool teachers need a level of support in their work that a principal trained in elementary education cannot provide.

Along with the other preschool teachers in their district, Chris, Jenny, and David receive the support of early childhood coaches. These coaches advance teachers' efforts to get the most out of the prescribed curricula and help identify opportunities for going off script to follow the children's interests. They help teachers reflect on their practice and listen more closely to their charges. The coaches provide the collegiality and mentorship to help novice teachers become more expert. They create learning communities for those who may be the only preschool teacher in a school building by organizing cross-school seminars on teaching and learning.

Organization

Self-contained classrooms. Jenny feels she is stealing time when her children participate in the flight curriculum. Chris bemoans the fact that there is not time for children to tell stories every day, the schedule that would provide the maximum benefits from this activity. David describes his schedule as a "bulldozer that plows over a child's joy and interest in a task or activity of his or her own choosing." Although there are several culprits here (too much testing, lack of flexibility in the required curriculum), one cause that must be remedied is the elementary school practice of pulling children out of class-rooms to be taught "specials" (e.g., art, music, physical education).

This model works well for children in elementary grades, enriching school experiences and allowing teachers important planning time (required in many union contracts). The model is problematic for preschoolers. Young children need long blocks of time to promote learning. Transitions from one activity or space to another can be trying in and of themselves. Young children do not readily return to a task once interrupted (especially if that return is 45 minutes later); they cannot simply be directed to "pick up where you left off."

Moreover, there is usually little benefit to children in these special classes. Preschool classrooms should already be stocked with art materials, and singing should be a regular feature of young children's days. While 4-year-olds need extensive gross motor activities, they are too young to participate in games with rules (making most physical education activities pointless). There is no evidence that a once-a-week Spanish class will have any benefit to a 3-year-old. With specialist teachers having little or no training in early childhood, art and music can become management nightmares that no one enjoys.

It goes without saying that teachers should be compensated for planning time (and because of the material-rich nature of the curriculum, preschool teachers require much time for preparation). However, preschools attached to a public school require a different model for designing that time.

NAEYC accreditation for all public school preschools. NAEYC accreditation standards are based on the best science and practice available from the field. Gaining accreditation requires developmentally appropriate curriculum (which includes play), sensitive and responsive teaching, and evaluation techniques that respect the rights of children. Accreditation can be used as a tool to promote and ensure high-quality programs.

Create strong early childhood departments. In describing the pressures of American education that lead to a pushdown of elementary practices to pre-school, in no way do we want to imply that those who run public schools hold some malice against young children. But because of these pressures, protective structures must be in place to ensure that preschool is done right. All school districts with preschools should have an early childhood depart-ment empowered with hiring teachers, creating curriculum, and directing policies. Although this department should draw on the expertise of other departments (math, literacy, science) to ensure that the learning of young childhood is driven by children's needs rather than by the desire to prepare children for specific, content-related standardized tests, the ultimate decisions about curriculum should be coordinated and controlled by early childhood educators.

Kindergarten should be included under the purview of early childhood departments. Although children are more capable at age 5 than they are at age 4, they are still very much young children (Copple & Bredekamp, 2008). They are squarely in the midst of what Erik Erikson (1968) describes as the time of initiative rather than industry. Most kindergartners (as opposed to their elementary school counterparts) are interested in trying things out, playing at writing and reading and soccer, and are not overly concerned about doing things right. In a year they will be ready and motivated to sit down in reading groups and begin learning the important tools of our culture. For now, they are still very much players rather than practicers.

Support for kindergarten to stand with preschool comes from an extensive review of primary education in England. This review concludes that children should not start formal learning until they are age 6. Kindergartners should continue with play-based curriculum. The report finds no reason to rush. Starting early does not mean greater success later on, and there is a risk that 5-year-olds introduced to formal curriculum too early will become turned off to academics (Alexander, 2009). Kindergartners should be accorded the full rights of early childhood.

There is great potential in preschools located in public schools. Offering salaries at more than double other types of early education, public schools have the ability to attract the very best early childhood educators, creating outstanding models of education and care for young children. If done right, with an eye toward respecting children's rights, public school preschools can become, like the best of community child care centers, a gift to children and their families (Mardell, 2002).

Notes

1   Our thanks to Jason Sachs, Ben Russell, and Mara Krechevsky for their comments on early drafts of this chapter. However, the opinions expressed here are solely are own.

2   Changes in regulations will allow preschool to be funded by this federal Department of Education program.

3   $500 million in Race to the Top Early Learning Challenge grants were awarded to nine states (California, Delaware, Maryland, Massachusetts, Minnesota, North Carolina, Ohio, Rhode Island and Washington) in December 2011.

References

Alexander, R. (2009). Children, their world and their education: Final report of the Cambridge primary review. Available at http://www.primaryreview.org.uk/Publications/Publications home.html

Alliance for Childhood. (2009). Crisis in the kindergarten: Why children need to play in schools. Available at http://www.allianceforchildhood.org

Barnett, W., & Masse, L. (2007). Comparative benefit-cost analysis of the Abecedarian program and its policy implications. *Economics of Education Review*, 26, 113–125.

Barnett, W., Hustedt, J., Friedman, A., Boyd, J., & Ainsworth, P. (2007). *The state of preschool: 2007 state preschool yearbook*. Camden, NJ: National Institute for Early Education Research.

Barnett, W., Robin, K., Hustedt, J., & Schulman, K. (2003). *The state of preschool: 2003 state preschool yearbook*. Camden, NJ: National Institute for Early Education Research.

Benson, B. (2008, August 26). N.H. is poised to offer kindergarten to all. Retrieved January 12, 2010, from http://www.boston.com/news/education/k_12/articles/2009/08/26/new_hampshire_becomes_last_state_to_offer_kindergarten_to_all_students/

Bronson, M. B. (2000, March). Recognizing and supporting the development of self-regulation in young children. *Young Children*, 55(2), 32–37.

Bruner, J. (1986). *Actual minds, possible worlds*. Cambridge, MA: Harvard University Press.

Bureau of Labor Statistics, U.S. Department of Labor. (2006). *Occupational outlook handbook*, 2010–11 edition, Bulletin 2800. Washington, DC: U.S. Government Printing Office.

Carlsson-Paige, N. (2008). *Taking back childhood: Helping your kids thrive in a fast-paced, media saturated, violence-filled world*. New York: Penguin Books.

Chaudhuri, A., & Potepan, M. (2009). *Key to economic success in the 21st century: Investment in early childhood programs*. San Francisco, CA: Bay Area Council.

Copple, C., & Bredekamp, S. (Eds.). (2008). *Developmentally appropriate practice in early childhood programs* (3rd ed.). Washington, DC: National Association for the Education of Young Children.

Deming, D., & Dynarski, S. (2008). The lengthening of childhood. *Journal of Economic Perspectives*, 22(3), 71–92.

Erikson, E. (1968). *Identity, youth and crisis*. New York: Norton.

Fuller, B. (2007). *Standardized childhood: The political and cultural struggle over early education*. Stanford, CA: Stanford University Press.

Harms, T., Clifford, R. M., & Cryer, D. (1998). *Early childhood environment rating scale–Revised*. New York: Teachers College Press.

Hartigan, P. (2009, August 30). Pressure cooker kindergarten. *Boston Globe Magazine*, pp. 24–28.

Herzenberg, S., Price, M., & Bradley, D. (2005). *Losing ground in early childhood education: Declining workforce qualifications in an expanding industry.* Washington, DC: Economic Policy Institute.

Katz, L., & Chard, S. (1989). *Engaging children's minds: The project approach.* Norwood, NJ: Albex.

Kinney, L. (2005). Small voices...powerful messages. In A. Clark, P. Moss, & A. Kjorholt (Eds.), *Beyond Listening: Children's perspectives on early childhood services* (pp. 111–128). Bristol, England: The Policy Press.

Kohn, A. (2001). Fighting the test: Turning frustration into action. Retrieved January 14, 2010, from http://www.alfiekohn.org/articles.htm

Mardell, B. (2002). *Growing up in child care.* Portsmouth, NH: Heinemann.

McCabe, A., Boccia, J., Bennett, M., Lyman, N., & Hagen, R. (2009). Improving oral language and literacy skills in preschool children from disadvantaged backgrounds: Remembering, writing and reading (RWR). Unpublished manuscript.

Mission Readiness. (2009). Military leaders for kids, ready, willing, and unable to serve. Retrieved on January 12, 2010, from http://cdn.missionreadiness.org/NATEE1109.pdf

National Association for the Education of Young Children. (2003). *Position statements on early childhood curriculum, assessment and program evaluation: Building an effective, accountable system in programs for children birth through age 8.* Washington, DC: Author.

National Center for Education Statistics. (2009). *The children born in 2001 at kindergarten entry: First findings from the kindergarten data collections of the early childhood longitudinal study, birth cohort (ECLS-B).* Washington, DC: U.S. Department of Education.

Pew Center on the States (2010). Votes count: Legislative action on pre-K fiscal year2011. Available at www.pewcenteronthestates.org/report_detail.aspx?id=62306

Pink, D. (2009) *Drive: The surprising truth about what motivates us.* New York: Penguin Books.

Project Zero & Reggio Children. (2001). *Making learning visible: Children as individual and group learners.* Reggio Emilia, Italy: Reggio Children.

Rinaldi, C. (2001). A pedagogy of listening. *Young Children in Europe*, 1, 2–5.

Salary.com. Parking lot attendant salaries. Retrieved January 12, 2010, from http://swz.salary.com/salarywizard/layouthtmls/swzl_compresult_national_SC16000189.html

Schekendanz, J., & Dickenson, D., 2003. *Open the world of learning.* Upper Saddle River, NJ: Pearson.

Schweinhart, L., Barnes, H., & Weikart, D. (1993). *Significant benefits: The High/Scope Perry Preschool Program study through age 27.* Ypsilanti, MI: High/Scope Press.

Snow, C., Porche, M., Tabors, P., & Harris, S. (2007). *Is literacy enough?* Baltimore, MD: Brookes.

Vygotsky, L. (1978). *Mind in society: The development of higher psychological processes.* Cambridge, MA: Harvard University Press.

West, J., Meek, A., & Hurst, D. (2000). *Children who enter kindergarten late or repeat kindergarten: Their characteristics and later school performance.* Retrieved January 12, 2010, from http://www.nces.ed.gov

Wilson, D. (2008). When worlds collide: Universal pre-K brings new challenges for public elementary schools. *Harvard Education Letter,* 24(6).

Young, M. (2009). Pre[k] now. Retrieved December 23, 2009, from www.preknow.org

❖ PART II ❖

Overview

The three chapters in Part II examine teacher education and professional development and advocate reskilling teacher candidates, in-service teachers, and K-12 students. As ways to reskill them, the chapters suggest changing the view of teacher candidates of a child, respecting teachers' voices, and promoting teacher collaboration in meeting the needs of students. Terri Swim, in "School Readiness and the Power of Documentation: Changing the Public Image to See the 'Rich Child'" (Chapter 3), notes that many teacher candidates initially tend to view a child with a "needy" perspective. Such a view results in more teacher-controlled instructions and more restrictions on the child's learning, and so it would deskill the children as well as the teachers themselves. The "rich" perspective on a child would lead teachers to take more positive attitudes toward children and treat them with greater compassion, expectations, and respect as they work with developing children. As a tool for a conceptual change, Swim introduces the method of documentation and shows how powerful the language used in preparing teachers can be in shaping their perceptions of what student–teacher interactions should look like. She also demonstrates how reflective practices can go a long way toward helping teachers to see the value that kids bring to the classroom with them and engaging them in ways that seek to transform rather than contain them. Her idea and method of reskilling are particularly important in that clearly what occurs in the classroom is a function of the preparation that occurs among educators outside the classroom.

Zeynep Isik-Ercan, in "Teachers Reclaiming Their Voices in Student Learning and Initiating Their Own Professional Growth: Suggestions for the Obama Administration" (Chapter 4), makes a strong argument for the need for teachers to have a voice in the preparation and collaboration that occur outside the classroom. By allowing teachers to be reflective on their practices in the public discourse without the harsh rhetoric that can stifle voices, we can create the communities of practice that our teachers and students need to be successful. Allowing teachers to express their voices freely would also empower teachers and help them engage in the process of reskilling their students and improving their own instructional practices.

Jane Leatherman, Nancy Bangel, Tracy Cox, Amber Merrill, and Rebecca Newsome, in "Teacher Collaborations Provide an Opportunity to Improve Education for All Students Along the Continuum of Learning" (Chapter 5), remind us to take a step back and examine the big picture related to attempts to create a "one-size-fits-all" education for students with varying and unique characteristics. For many, this represents a restrictive setting that can actually hamper their attempts at reaching their fullest potentials, and even worse it would end up deskilling—depriving students of opportunities of utilizing and honing their skills. Leatherman and her colleagues demonstrate how collaboration reskills teachers and expands the capabilities of teachers to adjust to the needs of an increasingly diverse student population.

Education not only refers to what happens inside the classroom, it also involves a complex social system beyond the classroom, such as teacher education and professional development practices. When we are hoping and striving for better education, we need to work on not only improving current teaching practices but also providing better training for our teacher candidates and more support for teacher collaboration. When our future teachers have more affirmative views on children, all teachers' voices are heard, and their collaborations are valued, we can be certain that we have a true hope for our future education.

CHAPTER THREE

School Readiness and the Power of Documentation: Changing the Public Image to See the "Rich Child"

Terri Jo Swim

Our current educational climate is polarized by two competing perspectives of the child. One regards children as being "rich," whereas the predominant view sees them as "needy." These views are entangled in how we judge the readiness of children for public schools. These divergent perspectives create a context for teacher educators that is fraught with tension about how to prepare preservice teachers for the "real classroom." This project investigates preliminary impacts of documentation on preservice teachers' reflections on their image of the child. The results suggest that teacher educators should join with allies to challenge preservice teachers', family members', and the public's image of the child to move the current educational discourse toward the "rich child" perspective.

President Obama and U.S. Secretary of Education Arne Duncan have explicitly stated their goals for early childhood education as the transformation of "early learning from a system of uneven quality and access into a system that truly and consistently prepares children for success in school and in life" (Duncan, 2009). Much emphasis and funding, via stimulus funds to Early Head Start and Head Start, for example, have focused on closing the achievement gap before public school entrance by requiring early education programs "to monitor and dramatically improve outcomes for young children" (Duncan, 2009). In other words, early education programs must be able to prove that children leave their care more ready for school than when they entered. Although I am not opposed to measuring the growth and development of young children following guidelines for appropriate assessment (National Association for the Education of Young Children, 2003), I fear that the current conceptualization of terms such as school readiness and assessment support a specific view of the child that takes us further away from reaching the president's goals both as an informed public and as a profession. In this chapter, I challenge the current image of the child and articulate ways in which a different view will propel the conversation forward and provide hope for demonstrating how each child is a competent and capable learner. To do so, we must lay a foundation for understanding what is already known about school readiness.

School Readiness

School readiness has been defined, traditionally, as the assessment and comparison of specific skills for individual children against a set of standard expectations or desired attributes (Dockett & Perry, 2009). Most school readiness assessments measure separate, isolated academic skills. Some assessments have expanded beyond academic skills to measure behavioral, social, or emotional skills. One of the major issues involved with measuring school readiness as isolated skills is the lack of predictive power into early elementary. La Paro and Pianta (2000) reported in their meta-analysis of 70 longitudinal studies that, on average, readiness assessments predicted 25% of variance in early school academic/cognitive performance and less than 10% of variance in social/behavioral measures in kindergarten, first, and second grades. Dockett and Perry (2007) state:

> Readiness assessments provide limited information about academic and social success in the first three years of school. Other factors—including what happens at school—account for the majority of variance after two to three years at school. (p. 32)

Thus, measures of school readiness that only focus on child characteristics tend to fall short in predictive power. More recently, alternative definitions of school readiness have been proposed to address this shortcoming. Carlton and Winsler (1999) called for a paradigm shift in the way school readiness was defined, carried out in practices, and measured. These authors argued for the inclusion of Vygotsky's sociocultural theory and other transactional theories of human development when defining the construct of school readiness. Doing so acknowledges a dialectical, complex, and ongoing process where children's biology and sociocultural environments exert reciprocal influences to co-create development (Carlton & Winsler, 1999).

Dockett and Perry (2009) explicitly expand this definition further when they state that school readiness is the complex interactions among children and their families, schools, and communities. From these perspectives, measuring child characteristics is only a small part of the school readiness puzzle. Characteristics of the family, school, and community (including access to health services and quality early childhood programs) must be assessed and accounted for as well.

Although these are important improvements in thinking about school readiness, neither definition goes far enough into the public realm to result in modified attitudes regarding the concept. Dahlberg, Moss, and Pence (1999) warn that

> The concept of early childhood education as a *foundation* for lifelong learning or the view that the early childhood institution contributes to children being *ready to learn* by the time they start school, produces a "poor" child in need of preparation before they can be expected to learn, rather than a "rich" child capable of learning from birth, whose learning during early childhood is one part of a continuous process of lifelong learning, no more nor less valid and important than other parts. (p. 83; italics original)

In the next sections, an argument is created for the purposeful inclusion of the image of the child into our understanding of school readiness, and one strategy, documentation, is explained as a tool for changing how teachers, families, and community members regard the work of young children.

Image of the Child

Each person holds an image of the child that is influenced by her own experiences, identity, and society that she inhabits. This image enables a person to recognize or not recognize certain qualities, value or devalue particular characteristics, and support or deny the potential of children (Rinaldi, 2001). For Italian educators in the city of Reggio Emilia, the image of the child includes the child as rich in resources, strong, and competent in learning and communicating with all of the hundred languages; they each have preparedness, potential, curiosity, and interest in relationships and constructing knowledge (Gandini, 2004; Rinaldi, 1998, 2001). For these educators, children are also viewed as challenging because they not only respond to the systems in which they are involved, including their families, society, and schools, but they also produce changes in them; they are producers of culture not just recipients of it (Rinaldi, 2001). From this image of the child, teachers must find tools to actively communicate with others regarding the children's capabilities, ways of thinking, and theory construction. When such knowledge is released beyond the school walls, community members are able to develop their own "rich" image of the child. The cultural and political value of sharing and dialoguing about the work of young children should not be underestimated because such democratic participation "is a common journey which makes it possible to construct the sense of belonging to a community" (Rinaldi, 2006, p. 175).

Although current calls for reform in education are toward more child-centered practices, this trend is by no means new (e.g., Dewey, 1916). Child-centered practices are sporadic in today's early childhood and public school classrooms. Carlina Rinaldi (2006) elaborates on this educational dilemma when she states:

> Much has been said and written about the competent child (who has the ability to learn, love, be moved, and live), the child who has a wealth of potentials, the powerful child in relation to what s/he is and can be right from birth. In practice, however, very little has been done that takes this image seriously. (p. 105)

The prevailing view of the child is not of the "rich" child but rather continues to be the "needy" child (Moss, Dillon, & Statham, 2000). In fact, U.S. legislation has fueled and further engrained this belief system for many adults. The No Child Left Behind (NCLB) Act of 2001, which receives continued support by President Obama, embraces and reinforces the "needy" child perspective through the focus on accountability, standardized testing, achievement gap, and school readiness (Armstrong, 2006), all of which are used and implemented from a "needy" child perspective.

The "needy" child perspective, in contrast to the "rich" image just discussed, looks at children as being weak, immature, and incomplete human beings who must rely on others to learn (Moss, Dillon, & Statham, 2000). In other words, they are viewed as being incapable of becoming educated and developing cognitively on their own; they must be taught (passively) all important knowledge by adults. To make such an image even more troubling, children are often viewed as categories (e.g., ready for school or not) rather than as individuals with unique strengths and abilities; minority and/or low-income children are seen as being the most unprepared for school and thus in need of special intervention (Cross & Swim, 2006). Hence, some children are labeled as "needy" simply by virtue of what characteristics they possess or what demographics they or their family represent. In other words, traditional and more contemporary conceptualizations of school readiness can result in measuring specific child, family, and community characteristics to determine school readiness, supporting the view of specific groups of children as "needy." Thus, what is important here is distinguishing when adults use the data gathered to uphold their "needy" image of the child and their decision-making power to devalue and marginalize particular groups of children (Dahlberg & Moss, 2006).

Assessment

As any educator or politician will attest to, assessment is a key component of how to make educational decisions and demonstrate accountability. The two images of the child discussed earlier are used to distinguish assessment practices and policies.

"Needy" Child and Standardized Testing

Policy mandates of pedagogies and assessments often work on an inherent mistrust of teachers (Lingard & Mills, 2007). Teachers are often viewed in the same "needy" fashion as the children (Swim & Merz, 2010), communicating a lack of faith in them as professionals. When teachers are viewed as lacking aptitude and capabilities, they cannot be trusted to be objective (Córdova, Hudson, Swank, Matthiesen, & Bertels, 2009). Thus, "assessment or its narrower companion, [standardized] testing" (Lingard & Mills, 2007, p. 237) becomes the primary driver of the educational system.

Standardized tests are viewed as the primary source of external validation of what was taught (and learned) in schools through the United States. These tests, designed by external experts, administered by "biased" teachers, and scored by "unbiased" graders, are used to measure knowledge attainment for all children at the same time. The problems associated with measuring teaching and learning through standardized tests have been well established in the literature, with some authors arguing that such assessment techniques violate the rights of young children (Mardell, Fiore, Boni, & Tonachel, 2010). The scope of this chapter is not to delve into those reasons but rather to discuss how the results of standardized tests are used for making educational decisions.

When children do not meet the cutoff score and are labeled as not ready for school, several outcomes can result. First, they can be given the "gift of time" by keeping them out of kindergarten if they are age-eligible (Graue, Kroeger, & Brown, 2003). Second, they might be placed in a classroom designed especially for children who are not ready for school (i.e., a developmental classroom). Third, they might be referred for further testing to see whether they qualify for special intervention services. As the last two options suggest, children who are not found ready for school may receive additional educational supports to assist them with gaining important knowledge and skills. All of these options ultimately put limitations on the child's potential because of the adult expectations that are created by this process of assessment. Research has found that teacher perceptions of their relationships with children predicted their perceptions of the children's academic ability above and beyond the children's actual measured achievement (Hughes, Gleason, & Zhang, 2005). In other words, how teachers think about particular children influences their perceptions and evaluations of academic abilities. If teachers see children as "needy," they will tend to treat them in a way that is consistent with that belief. The same pattern is true for teachers who see children as "rich."

"Rich" Child and Documentation

Teachers working within a "rich" child image value closely examining the work of the children in situ. In other words, they want to know how the child is building relationships between ideas and people, constructing knowledge, and developing theories. In order to really know young children, teachers have to be subjective co-learners. Their biases, just like researchers', must be acknowledged, explained, and used as part of the analysis. Thus, teachers use the pedagogy of listening and documentation to aid in the understanding of young children and the teaching-learning process.

The pedagogy of listening distinguishes the municipal preschools of Reggio Emilia, Italy, from other educational approaches (Rinaldi, 2001) because of the way the term listening is defined. Listening is about having the openness and sensitivity to hear with our eyes, ears, intellect, and emotions (Milikan, 2001) the hundred languages, symbols, and codes used to express ideas and feelings (Rinaldi, 2001). Listening is an active verb that involves interpreting messages, making sense and meaning, forming connections, and constructing and co-constructing understanding (Milikan, 2001; Rinaldi, 2001). Teachers must learn to listen to the children judiciously.

For accuracy, however, listening must be supported with evidence. Listening must progress from being an invisible part of a teacher's job to a visible trace in the environment; this is accomplished via documentation (Forman & Fyfe, 1998; Gandini & Goldhaber, 2001; Kroeger & Cardy, 2006; Rinaldi, 2001; Swim, 2005, 2007). Documentation provides evidence of listening—it is the traces that make visible the children's and teachers' learning. Documentation is not merely observing or the recording of observations for later assessment; it is the construction and reconstruction of events, learning, and interpretations through the use of transcriptions, slides, photographs, work samples, and videos (Gandini & Goldhaber, 2001; Merz & Swim, 2006; Rinaldi, 2001; Swim, 2007). When documentation is prepared, it is used for understanding as well as being understood because it provides insight into the children's as well as the teachers' work (Gandini & Goldhaber, 2001). The documentation becomes a "tool of the mind" for remembering, reflecting, revisiting, and learning and relearning as new ideas are explored in relation to the old ones (Forman, 1999; Forman & Fyfe, 1998; Hong & Broderick, 2003; Rinaldi, 1998). Documentation, then, not only provides a memory trace of past and current ideas, but it also sparks new ideas and, therefore, new directions for learning.

Documentation has been shown to be a valuable learning tool for children and adults. Research (Cross & Swim, 2006; Hong & Trepanier-Street, 2004) demonstrates that children could be responsible for making documentation and utilizing it to guide their work. For example, children would visit the documentation panel created from a child's writing when making their own product from found materials (Cross & Swim, 2006). In addition, children would view each other's photographic slide shows and have conversations with each other when they encountered a problem they could not solve independently. In other words, the children used each other and the documentation as resources to facilitate and sustain their work (Cross & Swim, 2006). Children can also view and re-view a video of their work to gain a new perspective of their work, the work of others, and to reflect on their strategies for problem solving (Forman, 1999; Hong & Broderick, 2003).

Documentation has been implemented primarily by teachers to explain the learning and development of the young children in their classrooms (see e.g., Edwards, Gandini, & Forman, 1998) and to inform the creation of a responsive, meaningful curriculum that supports and facilitates learning for each child (Cross & Swim, 2006; Hughes, 2002) because "documentation embodies the essence of getting closer to children's thinking" (Kroeger & Cardy, 2006, p. 391). However, educators in Italy also use it to facilitate the development of adult learners (see e.g., Project Zero, 2003). Recently, teacher educators in the United States have begun to document the learning that is occurring for preservice teachers in college classrooms to assist with reflective practices (Goldhaber & Smith, 2002; Hong & McNair, 2003; Warash, 2005) as well as the acquisition of knowledge and dispositions (e.g., understanding and valuing developmentally appropriate practice) (Swim, 2007).

Kroeger and Cardy (2006) suggest that learning to document is a challenging task for preservice teachers because it demands that they make a philosophical shift toward child-centered, constructivist practices. Moreover, this often has to be done in educational contexts that do not support such a shift (i.e., preservice teachers engage in field experiences with teachers or programs that use policies and practices that support the "needy" child image). In other words, teacher educators face the centuries-old educational dilemma: How do teacher educators help preservice teachers move toward practices that run counter to prevailing practices in early childhood programs and public schools?

Context for Teacher Educators

Teacher educators find themselves in a context fraught with tension about how to best prepare their preservice teachers for the "real world of the classroom" because of the continuum of possible beliefs and practices separating the "needy child" and the "rich child" perspectives. Although the "rich" child perspective might direct current research and the university curriculum, the "needy" child perspective, more than likely, dominated preservice teachers' educational experiences when they attended elementary, middle school, and high school. Moreover, it is highly likely that the schools and/or teachers in their current field experiences espouse such practices because this perspective is "almost universally embraced" in education (Armstrong, 2006, p. 3). Thus, the "needy" child perspective is familiar, comfortable, and mostly unexamined by them.

Evidence is mounting that adult learners (i.e., preservice and in-service teachers) must be provided with provocative experiences that cause careful reflection on their approach to education if they are going to think differently about the capabilities of young children as well as alternative methods for facilitating learning (see e.g., Edwards, Gandini, & Forman, 1998; Schon, 1995). Adult learners must be provided with powerful opportunities to construct knowledge about listening and the image of the child (Swim, 2005), the role of the teacher when focusing on children's learning (Linek, Fleener, Fazio, Raine, & Klakamp, 2003; Swim, 2005), and developmentally appropriate practices (Swim, 2007). Teacher educators must learn to "apply what we know about how children learn to understand how adults learn … [so we can uncover] … how to best teach in ways that facilitate learning in our adult students" (Chaille, 1997, p. 23). In this way, we must also recognize how our image of the learner (i.e., preservice teachers) impacts our own behavior in the classroom. Loris Malaguzzi suggests that we often do not give enough credit to the potential that all learners possess when he says:

> We must be convinced that children, like us, have stronger powers than those we have been told about, powers which we all possess—us and the children, stronger potential than we give them credit for. We must understand how, without even realizing it, we make so little use of the energy potential within each of us. (cited in Rinaldi, 2006, p. 55)

To apply this thesis in undergraduate courses, teacher educators must believe that preservice teachers are capable of engaging in the philosophical debate involving these perspectives and addressing where their pedagogical beliefs and values are located on the "needy" child–"rich" child continuum. We must also believe that they are able to extend beyond their previous experiences as students to adopt the profession's current thinking about children and learning.

In the next section, I explore a multiyear investigation that I conducted with my undergraduate students. I wanted to investigate, among other questions, how engaging in a semester-long documentation project impacted their thinking about the capabilities of young children. The data provide one example of how providing provocative experiences to spark reflection might be useful as teacher educators, how we might develop hope for possible ways of impacting educators and community members' images of the child.

Documentation and the "Rich" Child Investigation

In one of my undergraduate courses, I investigated how creating an engaging course-long documentation project impacted the preservice teachers' reflections regarding their image of the child. Of the 112 preservice teachers enrolled in my course over the course of five semesters, 101 preservice teachers provided data for this study. All data collection occurred during regularly scheduled class times and was approved by the Internal Review Board on Human Subjects.

Each preservice teacher was required, as part of this course, to complete between 15 and 35 hours of field experience with preschool or kindergarten children in a local urban school district. The preservice teachers were required to gather observational data each time they participated in their field experience. The data consisted of anecdotal records, running records, photographs, and/or work samples. Preservice teachers were asked to observe during three to four field experiences and then identify a question with their field partner that they wanted to investigate. This joint question was to reflect observations or ideas that they were currently wondering about regarding their work with children. The purpose of having them pose a research question was, on the one hand, arbitrary because documentation does not always start from a single point or question; for seasoned teachers, it often emerges from the data gathered and reflects the ongoing process of learning for teachers and children. On the other hand, without a focus, preservice teachers struggled to balance the demands of teaching; documentation was viewed as distracting them from other valuable teacher duties (e.g., classroom management) rather than a new tool for organizing and facilitating their work (Kroeger & Cardy, 2006).

Preservice teachers were then required to create a documentation panel explaining their question for investigation as well as what they learned from the children, teachers, or program. After the documentation panels were created but before they were shared as a class, I asked them to individually complete four reflection questions:

1. How did the process of gathering observational data during your field experience help you to learn to listen to the children?
2. While designing/creating the documentation, what did you think about/consider regarding the children and their capabilities?
3. How does documenting learning in this manner help you to think about the relationships among teaching, learning, and assessment?
4. What did you learn about your abilities to document learning over the course of this semester?

Although a great deal could be learned from all of their answers to these questions, the following section only addresses how the documentation influenced their thinking about the children's capabilities (e.g., their image of the child). The author read all answers and classified them into categories based on similarities in responses. Then, each group was reread for consistency in coding. In the end, eight categories representing different thoughts about the capabilities of the children were formed. In general, the experience of documenting learning positively impacted how the preservice teachers thought about the capabilities of children.

Table 3.1: Categories of Answers When Preservice Teachers Were Asked About the Capabilities of Young Children

Category	Frequency (%) ($n = 101$)	Sample Quote
Changed ideas about capabilities	22 (22)	[I began to] look at the children differently. I realized the strengths of the children…
Children were highly capable	8 (8)	I considered that children have a lot of knowledge and we need to help the children bring out what they know.
Discussed child environment impacts on capabilities	9 (9)	I was interested in how the children adapted to the changes in their environment as well as how they changed things to suit their needs.
Growth in capabilities	10 (10)	I recognized everyone's particular learning level. If I noticed a child was improving even though they may not have been at a level someone else was at I would still document this improvement.
Discussed children's current level of capabilities	26 (26)	I thought a lot about their communication skills and working together.
Raised questions about children's capabilities	1 (1)	It really raised more questions for me than it answered.
No direct mention of children's capabilities	22 (22)	It made me realize what they were learning and what that meant.
Children were not capable	3 (3)	I realized that I was expecting too much from the children. They all did not know their alphabet, so how could I expect them to be writing and reading during their free centers? I was thinking beyond their skills.

Table 3.1 shows that 22 of the preservice teachers specifically mentioned changing their ideas (e.g., "I realized...) about the capabilities of the children over the course of the semester-long documentation project. They noticed that the children were more capable than they or other adults might give them credit for. Some additional sample quotes from this group include:

- I was blown away when watching the children, how in depth they could get, as well as how they put themselves out there, open to learning something new. The children and their capabilities are always greater than what we give them credit for.

- I was amazed at the accomplishments even the youngest (3-year-old) child could do. I know if you give children an opportunity to grow and learn they will surprise you in their accomplishments. Similarly, a second student said: I noticed that even children as young as 3 or 4 are capable of a lot more than I gave them credit for originally. They know what they want to learn and are very self-sufficient.

- So often I see adults dismissing what their children are saying as just "child talk." But if you really listen to what they say, you can get a better grasp of how they are constructing knowledge.

- I have been working with young children for a long time [as a preschool teacher and center director], but I was amazed by the children's capabilities. Because of the observations and data collected, I realized that the children were able to make wise choices when given the chance to do so.

These responses clearly reflected how preservice teachers hold a nascent image of the child as "rich" in capabilities and resources. Their answers also provided evidence that many of them have altered previous ideas about children as they spoke of specific changes in their beliefs and how "we" or "adults" tend to view children. This language suggested that they were able to identify the prevailing conceptualizations about children and their capabilities (i.e., "needy child" perspective) but were in the process of transitioning to a new way of understanding young children (e.g., "rich child" perspective).

Another group of eight preservice teachers discussed how the children were highly capable. They did not indicate in any way whether these were old or new ideas for themselves, so they were analyzed separately from the previous category. Regardless of whether these quotes represent a change in thinking, the preservice teachers have established the important concept: a positive image of the child. Sample quotes for this group include:

- Once given the chance to expand their mind, children can come up with solutions and answers and can learn the concepts of any subject matter.
- They are smart.
- Children are very capable and intelligent.

Preservice teachers also commented on how the environment impacted the children's capabilities and how the children shaped the environment. For example, they commented, "I wanted to show that the children are learning with the art materials, rather than playing with them. They are learning to represent real life objects through the materials" and "When interest and social interactions were both present, children's capabilities were most expanded."

This category was intriguing because it represents how the students pulled other key concepts for the course into their "rich" image of the child. They considered the complex interactions between the environment created for and by children with the expression of child capabilities. Although none of the responses in this category openly claimed that the author had changed her image of the child, it is evident that the course impacted how it was being conceptualized positively around the capabilities of young children.

The next two categories of responses all discussed the children's current levels of capabilities. One group of preservice teachers did so when describing how they noticed growth in the children's capabilities throughout the semester, while the other mentioned considering the children's current level of capabilities while creating the documentation panels. Comments such as "I thought about the social skills the children were using" or "They did understand how to use their senses to observe and analyze" provide insight into the preservice teachers' thinking about the children's current skills.

Only three students openly stated that children were incapable or that they had overestimated the children's ability levels, while 22 students provided answers that lacked depth or clear connection to the question posed. The latter group of preservice teachers tended to focus broadly on learning or learning in relationship to a specific content area (e.g., math or literacy), rather than speak of specific competencies. Of course, this category may actually be larger due to social desirability. Some students may have wanted to impress me with an answer they thought was desirable given the course content (e.g., learning experiences and readings) rather than responding with their own beliefs about the capabilities of children.

In summary, engaging in this course-long documentation project positively impacted the image of the child for some students. Thirty-nine percent of the preservice teachers left the class holding an image of the child as very competent, with 31% providing evidence of how the course experiences and/or concepts had impacted their image. Another 36% of the group focused on either the children's current levels of competence or their growth in capabilities. In general, the outcomes of this study provide hope, albeit not uniform, for changing preservice teachers' images of the child through provocative learning experiences that spark reflection.

Limitations of Study

Documenting the learning of young children may prove to be a powerful tool for impacting preservice teachers' image of the child. This study, however, did not directly assess how these students thought about school readiness or assessment. It would be reasonable to hypothesize that altering one's image of the child would necessarily need to result in modifications in other aspects of their belief systems. Some questions to consider in future studies include: Do preservice teachers who possess a "rich" image of the child simultaneously hold the belief that children who do not possess particular characteristics associated with school readiness should be advised to not attend kindergarten even if age-eligible? Or, should categorical data gathered from standardized tests be viewed as more important when making educational decisions than documentation created by teachers in classrooms? More empirical research needs to be conducted to investigate these theoretical and dispositional links for preservice teachers.

Conclusions

The school reform literature (e.g., Newmann & Associates, 1996) emphasizes that teacher practices are central to effective school reform. This places particular responsibility on teacher educators to assume our rightful roles of educational leaders and assume the burden of responsibility for challenging the prevailing view of the "needy" child. We must seize control of issues within the accountability frame and articulate our directions for future changes. Teacher educators "must stop criticizing those who seek accountability and join them in developing *effective* measures of achievement that can be used to improve educational opportunities for *all* students" (Poplin & Rivera, 2005, p. 30; italics added). Teacher educators can begin by inventing, borrowing, or otherwise altering our practices to create meaningful experiences whereby preservice teachers are challenged to consider learner-centered practices (Brown, 2003) focusing on the capabilities of children. In this study, the preservice teachers' growth and understanding of the image of the "rich" child demonstrate the power of such experiences for facilitating learning. These preservice teachers altered their image of the child after experiencing the documentation project. Although this modification might have only been in the short run, Peterson, McCarthey, and Elmore (1996) point out, "Changing practice is primarily a problem of learning....Teachers who see themselves as learners work continuously to develop new understandings and improve their practices" (p. 148). It is my hope that this learning experience was powerful enough to cause the preservice teachers to continue learning about and using documentation to assess the authentic learning of young children in their future classrooms.

It is not sufficient to just create a rich learning experience in the college classroom. Teacher educators must also take the time to reflect with the students on the learning that occurred in the early childhood classroom as well as the college classroom. Revisiting documentation provided the time and space for the preservice teachers to pause and revisit classroom events and their impact on them as learners (Merz & Swim, 2006). If we change the way that we teach and develop a specific culture around assessing learning and challenging preservice teachers' thinking about young children (Swim, 2007), we may be able to move the current educational discourse away from the "needy" child perspective toward the "rich" child perspective.

The documentation experience may have been particularly influential in sparking movement toward a "rich" image of the child because of the population of children with whom these teachers worked. The predominately white, middle-class preservice teachers had different familial, cultural, and educational experiences than the children, who represented a great variety of racial/ethnic, cultural, and socioeconomic backgrounds. When teacher educators create challenging, meaningful learning opportunities to spark reflection on experiences with children who are different from the preservice teachers, images of each child as capable and competent can be created and re-created. Given the achievement gap that President Obama and others are concerned about closing, this may be the most promising outcome of this research because, as Delpit (2006) states,

> When teachers are committed to teaching all students, and when they understand
> that through their teaching change *can* occur, then the chance for transformation is
> great. (p. 166; italics original)

Teacher educators cannot be satisfied with short-term promises of instructional strategies when it comes to closing the achievement gap and achieving social justice in our education system. As key playes, teacher educators "must accept that the university has been as much a part of the system of education that has created achievement gaps as any other group, perhaps more so, and we must be radically prepared to try new things to change it" (Poplin & Rivera, 2005, p. 35). We should assume the responsibility for measuring and being held accountable for ensuring that the image of the "rich" child extends beyond mere words to being evident in the preservice teachers' behaviors and dispositions when working with children before and after graduation.

Although the role of meaningful experiences created by teacher educators should not be underestimated in helping preservice teachers to understand young children, the process cannot stop there. Teacher educators cannot accomplish systematic change in isolation. We need to join with allies to address educational issues such as assessment and school readiness at a multitude of levels with community members, administrators, teachers, and children. Studying and appropriating educational philosophies, systems, and practices in other countries (Merz & Glover, 2006; Swim & Merz, 2010) can assist in our better understanding of how to build the "rich" image of the child in family and community members. The educational leaders in Reggio Emilia, Italy, provide valuable instruction regarding ways to take the work of the children to the public (e.g., Edwards, Gandini, & Forman, 1998). In the early days of the programs, the teachers and children would take learning materials into the center of the city to do their work. They would set up easels, for example, so that community members could see the process of creating with paint.

I am suggesting that we literally and figuratively take the work of children to the community to intentionally build different types of "public pedagogies" (Giroux, 2004) that focus on the capabilities of young children. Watching children work should raise important questions about meaningful tasks, authentic assessments, and the purpose of education, just to name a few. Children and families are bombarded with public pedagogies that build particular identities—from billboards, music, sports media, and so on. We need to harness the power of public pedagogies to reclaim a message of competent children and teachers.

When it is not possible to take the children into the community to work, teachers can share the work indirectly through documentation. Carefully examining documentation allows community members to read the data (e.g., transcripts of conversations, work samples, photographs of process, products produced) provided to independently draw conclusions about the capabilities of young children, their "richness." As Forman and Fyfe (1998) suggest,

> Documentation panels make visible the work of the schools and the capacities of the children. Real examples of documented learning offer the public a more particular kind of knowledge that empowers and provokes them to reflect, question, and rethink or reconstruct the image of the child and the rights of children to quality education. (p. 256)

Early childhood teachers, public school teachers, and administrators must make concerted efforts to share documentation with families and community members in addition to the required sharing of the results of standardized tests. Placing both types of evidence side by side should invite many reactions, opinions, and open lines of communication as the data are analyzed and compared. For example, it should raise the question of social justice as examples of academic and developmental growth are placed along a measure of finite attainment. In addition, it may increase family and community members' emotional investments in the schools. Lewin-Benham (2006) found that when parents in her program were invited to dialogue through documentation, they felt valued as members of the educational process. Strong emotional ties might make it harder for family and community members to accept labels put on children, teachers, and schools such as "not ready" or "failing." In other words, they may come to see not only children as "rich" but also teachers and schools. Moving the conversation about children's learning and schools' performances into a public dialogue puts it where it rightfully belongs in a democratic society. Rinaldi (2006) states that:

> Documentation...offers a true experience of democracy because democracy also means exchange, and this exchange is made possible by the visibility and the recognition of differences and subjectivity. When differences and subjectivities are in dialogue, they become educational values that are not only declared but also lived. (p. 130)

When conversations advocating for a "rich" image of young children's capabilities move beyond the school walls, more people have opportunities to better understand and challenge both perspectives. As this image spreads further into the community, people should be invited to rethink the links among the "rich" image of the child, policies and practices regarding school readiness, and how we assess the learning and development of young children.

President Obama and U.S. Secretary of Education Arne Duncan want to move the field of education forward to minimize the achievement disparity based on race. Although this goal is noble, we cannot get there as a nation without changing the way educators and the public alike think about school readiness and the assessment of young children. Teacher educators can play a significant role in helping preservice teachers to rethink their image of the child. Yet we cannot act in isolation. We must join with our allies to engage in systematic changes. Documentation demonstrates a clear value of the children's work and acknowledges their capabilities; it is a pedagogical tool that "makes children want to learn and teachers want to teach" (Wien, 2008, p. 3). By joining together to address this problem, systematic educational changes can be realized for each young child in America.

References

Armstrong, T. (2006). *The best schools: How human development research should inform educational practice.* Alexandria, VA: Association for Supervision and Curriculum Development.

Brown, K. L. (2003). From teacher-centered to learner-centered curriculum: Improving learning in diverse classrooms. *Journal of Higher Education,* 124(1), 49–54.

Carlton, M. P., & Winsler, A. (1999). School readiness: The need for a paradigm shift. *School Psychology Review*, 28(3), 338–352.

Chaille, C. (1997). How does a constructivist teach teachers? *Journal of Early Childhood Teacher Education*, 18(2), 23–26.

Córdova, R. A., Jr., Hudson, J., Swank, P., Matthiesen, A., & Bertels, M. (2009). Reclaiming and composing our professional lives: A young writing project learns a language of inquiry to establish, thicken, and sustain its work. *Scholarlypartnershipsedu,* 4(2), 23–37.

Cross, D. J., & Swim, T. J. (2006). A scholarly partnership for examining the pragmatics of Reggio-inspired practice in an early-childhood classroom: Provocations, documentation, and time. *Scholarlypartnershipsedu*, 1(1), 47–68.

Dahlberg, G., & Moss, P. (2006). Introduction: Our Reggio Emilia. In C. Rinaldi (Ed.), *In dialogue with Reggio Emilia: Listening, researching, and learning* (G. Dahlberg & P. Moss, Series Eds.). London: Routledge.

Dahlberg, G., Moss, P., & Pence, A. (1999). *Beyond quality in early childhood education and care: Postmodern perspectives.* London: RoutledgeFalmer.

Delpit, L. (2006). *Other people's children: Cultural conflict in the classroom* (rev. ed.). New York: New Press.

Dewey, J. (1916). *Democracy and education: An introduction to the philosophy of education.* New York: Macmillan.

Dockett, S., & Perry, B. (2007). *Transitions to school: Perceptions, experiences and expectations.* Sydney: University of New South Wales Press.

Dockett, S., & Perry, B. (2009). Readiness for school: A relational construct. *Australasian Journal of Early Childhood*, 34(1), 20–26.

Duncan, A. (2009, November). The early learning challenge: Raising the bar. Opening remarks at the National Association for the Education of Young Children annual conference, Washington, DC. Retrieved March 8, 2010, from http://www2.ed.gov/news/speeches/2009/11/11182009.html.

Edwards, C., Gandini, L., & Forman, G. (Eds.). (1998). *The hundred languages of children: The Reggio Emilia approach—Advanced reflections.* Westport, CT: Ablex Publishing.

Forman, G. (1999). Instant video revisiting: The video camera as a "Tool of the Mind" for young children. *Early Childhood Research & Practice: An Internet Journal on the Development, Care, and Education of Young Children,* 1(2). Retrieved February 7, 2006, from http://ecrp.uiuc.edu/v1n2/forman.html.

Forman, G., & Fyfe, B. (1998). Negotiated learning through design, documentation, and discourse. In C. P. Edwards, L. Gandini, & G. Forman (Eds.), *The 100 languages of children: The Reggio Emilia approach—Advanced reflections* (2nd ed., pp. 239–260). Greenwich, CT: Ablex.

Gandini, L. (2004). Foundations of the Reggio Emilia approach. In J. Hendrick (Ed.), *Next steps towards teaching the Reggio way: Accepting the challenge to* change (2nd ed.). Upper Saddle River, NJ: Pearson Merrill Prentice Hall.

Gandini, L., & Goldhaber, J. (2001). Two reflections about documentation. In L. Gandini & C. P. Edwards (Eds.), *Bambini: The Italian approach to infant/toddler care* (pp. 124–145). New York: Teachers College Press.

Giroux, H. (2004). Public pedagogy and the politics of neo-liberalism: Making the political more pedagogical. *Policy Futures in Education,* 2(3–4), 494–503.

Goldhaber, J., & Smith, D. (2002). The development of documentation strategies to support teacher reflection, inquiry, and collaboration. In V. R. Fu, A. J. Stremmel, & L. T. Hill (Eds.), *Teaching and learning: Collaborative exploration of the Reggio Emilia Approach* (pp. 147–160). Upper Saddle River, NJ: Merrill Prentice Hall.

Graue, M. E., Kroeger, J., & Brown, C. (2003, Spring). The gift of time: Enactments of developmental thought in early childhood practice. *Early Childhood Research and Practice: An Internet Journal on the Development, Care, & Education of Young Children,* 5(1). Retrieved February 4, 2006, from http://ecrp.uiuc.edu/v5n1/graue.html.

Hong, S. B., & Broderick, J. T. (2003, Spring). Instant video revisiting for reflecting: Extending the learning of children and teachers. *Early Childhood Research & Practice: An Internet Journal on the Development, Care, and Education of Young Children,* 5(1). Retrieved February 7, 2006, from http://ecrp.uiuc.edu/v5n1/hong.html.

Hong, S. B., & McNair, S. (2003). Documentation in children's project work: A tool for fostering reflection and reconstruction in preservice and inservice teachers. Teaching strategies. *Journal of Early Education and Family Review,* 11(1), 35–42.

Hong, S. B., & Trepanier-Street, M. (2004). Technology: A tool for knowledge construction in a Reggio Emilia inspired teacher education program. *Early Childhood Education Journal,* 32(2), 87–94.

Hughes, E. (2002). Planning meaningful curriculum: A mini story of children and teachers learning together. *Childhood Education,* 78(3), 134–139.

Hughes, J. N., Gleason, K. A., & Zhang, D. (2005). Relationship influences on teachers' perceptions of academic competence in academically at-risk minority and majority first grade students. *Journal of School Psychology*, 43(4), 303–320.

Kroeger, J., & Cardy, T. (2006). Documentation: A hard place to reach. *Early Childhood Education Journal*, 33(6), 389–398.

La Paro, K., & Pianta, R. C. (2000). Predicting children's competence in the early school years: A meta-analytic review. *Review of Educational Research*, 70(4), 443–484.

Lewin-Benham, A. (2006). *Possible schools: The Reggio approach to urban education.* New York: Teachers College Press.

Linek, W. M., Fleener, C., Fazio, M., Raine, I. L., & Klakamp, K. (2003). The impact of shifting from "how to teach" to "how children learn." *Journal of Educational Research*, 97(2), 78–91.

Lingard, B., & Mills, M. (2007). Pedagogies making a difference: Issues of social justice and inclusion. *International Journal of Inclusive Education*, 11(3), 233–244.

Mardell, B., Fiore, L., Boni, M., & Tonachel, M. (2010). The rights of children: Policies to best serve three-, four- and five-year-olds in public schools. *Scholarlypartnershipsedu*, 5(1), 38–52.

Merz, A. H., & Glover, M. (2006). Are we there yet? One public school's journey in appropriating the Reggio Emilia Approach. *Scholarlypartnershipsedu*, 1(1), 28–46.

Merz, A. H., & Swim, T. J. (2006, October 13). Using technology to assess pre-service teachers' mathematical dispositions in situ. Invited presentation for the Division K meeting: Technology in Teaching and Research at the Midwest Educational Research Association (MWERA), Columbus, OH.

Milikan, J. (2001, July). Rejoicing in subjectivity. Paper presented at the sixth annual Unpacking Conference, Sydney, Australia.

Moss, P., Dillon, J., & Statham, J. (2000). The "child in need" and "the rich child": Discourses, constructions, and practice. *Critical Social Policy*, 20(2), 233–254.

National Association for the Education of Young Children. (2003). *Position statement: Early childhood curriculum, assessment, and program evaluation: Building an effective, accountable system in programs for children birth through age 8.* Washington, DC: Author.

Newmann, F., & Associates. (1996). *Authentic achievement: Restructuring schools for intellectual quality.* San Francisco, CA: Jossey-Bass.

Peterson, P. L., McCarthey, S. J., & Elmore, R. F. (1996). Learning from school restructuring. *American Educational Research Journal*, 33(1), 119–153.

Poplin, M., & Rivera, J. (2005, Winter). Merging social justice and accountability: Educating qualified and effective teachers. *Theory into Practice*, 44(1), 27–37.

Project Zero. (2003). *Making teaching visible: Documenting individual and group learning as professional development.* Cambridge, MA: Author.

Rinaldi, C. (1998). Projected curriculum constructed through documentation—Progettazione: An interview with Lella Gandini. In C. P. Edwards, L. Gandini, & G. Forman (Eds.), *The hundred languages of children: The Reggio Emilia approach—Advanced reflections* (2nd ed., pp. 113–125). Westport, CT: Ablex Publishing.

Rinaldi, C. (2001). Infant-toddler centers and preschools as places of culture. *In Project Zero and Reggio Children: Making learning visible: Children as individual and group learners* (pp. 38–46). Reggio Emilia, Italy: Reggio Children.

Rinaldi, C. (2006). *In dialogue with Reggio Emilia: Listening, researching, and learning.* In G. Dahlberg & P. Moss (Series Eds.), Contesting early childhood series. London: Routledge.

Schon, D. A. (1995). *The reflective practitioner: How professionals think in action.* Aldershot, England: Arena.

Swim, T. J. (2005). What role do teacher education programs play in creating the symphony of voices in educational settings? Paper presented as part of a symposium titled Coming Together in a Symphony of Voices: Authentic Documentation as Praxis for Assessing Learning at the 2005 AERA meeting, Montreal, Canada.

Swim, T. J. (2007). Documenting pre-service teachers' work: A tool for influencing reflections about developmentally appropriate practices. *Teacher Education and Practice,* 20(4), 376–394.

Swim, T. J., & Merz, A. H. (2010). Deconstructing assessment practices: Are our children "needy" or "rich" in possibilities? Manuscript submitted for publication.

Warash, B. G. (2005). Documentation panels enhance teacher education programs. Journal of *Early Childhood Teacher Education,* 26(4), 437–442.

Wien, C. A. (2008). *Emergent curriculum in the primary classroom: Interpreting the Reggio Emilia approach in schools.* New York: Teachers College Press.

CHAPTER FOUR

Teachers Reclaiming Their Voices in Student Learning and Initiating Their Own Professional Growth: Suggestions for the Obama Administration

Zeynep Isik-Ercan

What is the most important role of teachers? How do teachers respond to changes in educational policy? To what extent should teachers have autonomy for what they teach and how they will teach it? Questions like these have been haunting researchers and policymakers of public education in the United States since the establishment of formal schooling. Social, historical, economic, and political waves on local, national, and international scales have always influenced how teachers are prepared and should be prepared to teach. Hence, the role of teachers has been reconceptualized each time the purpose of education is defined by policy makers, as well as philosophers, educators, and researchers. Indeed, the education of teachers and the education of K-12 students have always been inextricably intertwined. Therefore, constant calls for educational reform since the 1980s, with the assumption that public schools fail and have always failed, have instantly reflected on the teachers and how they gain expertise in teaching; voices emerging countless times from researchers and policymakers, with the latter almost always heard more loudly (Sarason, 1990), that a change is needed in the way teachers are prepared to teach or the way they teach if we need to make educational change happen. Kumashiro (2010) highlights how it is interesting that instead of structural reforms to increase the quality of public schools, "needing more high-quality teachers" has been the motto of educational reform initiatives since No Child Left Behind (NCLB) was first launched. Recent public remarks made by President Obama and Secretary of Education Arne Duncan also echo this perspective. For instance, President Obama's roadmap summary to improve K-12 education on a 2008 presidential campaign website read:

> We will recruit an army of new teachers and develop innovative ways to reward teachers who are doing a great job, and we will reform No Child Left Behind so that we are supporting schools that need improvement, rather than punishing them. (Organizing for America, 2008)

Many times, however, teachers' voices are not heard in policymakers' description of such reform that dramatically impacts their personal and professional lives. Take the following excerpts from President Obama's remarks in March 2010:

> We'll not only challenge states to identify high schools with graduation rates below 60 percent, we're going to invest another $900 million in strategies to get those graduation rates up. Strategies like transforming schools from top to bottom by bringing in a new principal, and training teachers to use more effective techniques in the classroom. Strategies like closing a school for a time and reopening it under new management, or even shutting it down entirely and sending its students to a better school. (Obama, 2010)

As these dramatic strategies such as transforming schools by bringing in a new principal or closing a school are proposed, there is no evidence that these decisions will include teacher voices. Teachers are thought of as "specialists" who have to do their job "effectively" independently of social, economic, and cultural contexts and regardless of any changes in school administration and school community. Moreover, when President Obama mentions "training teachers to use more effective techniques in the classroom," ambivalence as to what constitutes an effective teacher stands out. One ironic example is how alternative and faster routes to teacher certification are sought as a way to recruit "effective" teachers, disregarding the need for teacher growth through rigorous clinical experiences.

In this chapter, I argue that teachers, in this challenging climate of mandated accountability without prerogative and entitlement, need to reclaim their voices by reconsidering their critical roles in the teaching and learning process. I suggest that teachers could take leadership in their own professional growth and engage in initiating reform that is teacher driven so that they could be empowered by the change and become its agents and not objects. I include implications and suggestions for teacher educators and policymakers in the Obama era to support this process.

Understanding the Role of Teachers in Schooling

Beyond political rhetoric, it is important to understand what it is that we expect our teachers to do before any definition of "effectiveness" is discussed. Understanding who teachers are begins with a simple question: What is expected from teachers? Perceptions about the role of teachers have been changing with the rapid transformations that the United States is going through. Although current attempts to measure teacher performance only include standardized test outcomes as an indicator of student learning, a broader look at the current goals of education as an institution is necessary. Orienting from a system that was expected to "produce" factory job skills, education now has higher demands for teachers, such as providing students with critical thinking and collaboration skills in a postindustrial knowledge society, preparing them for highly skilled jobs as well as for citizenship in a democratic society.

Theoretical understandings of the role of the teacher also vary with social, economic, and political changes the society went through, shaping the expectations for the qualifications of teachers. Therefore, teacher roles are contextual and historic to a given community, and teachers perceive these roles differently based on their local contexts and needs. For instance, Jalongo and Isenberg (1995) found that teachers' orientation toward teaching is intertwined with their perception of their power and care for students. *The public service orientation* to teaching is represented through "I am just a teacher" statement, implying carelessness and powerlessness. *The professional career orientation* to teaching is mirrored with "I am a teacher" statement and implies power through recognition by others and a focus on mastery in teaching. The highest level of orientation toward teaching is *role model orientation*, in which the teachers become confident and ready for challenges to life-long improvement in teaching and learning.

Various theoretical and philosophical understandings of teaching and learning are hidden in the discourses about teacher roles. Conceptual frameworks and pedagogies of different teacher education programs typically indicate the teacher roles they each envision. However, in the public debates and accounts by the Obama administration about what is expected of teachers, the desired outcomes for teachers are usually described (i.e., creating effective teachers), yet the means of accomplishing these goals, such as the specific changes in knowledge, skills, and dispositions of teachers, are often left vague. Many times issues and conflicts emerge as these roles are perceived differently by teachers, teacher educators, administrators, and policymakers. Because of this ambiguity, I first want to make explicit how different schools of thought describe teachers' role. I think through understanding how their roles could be crafted differently despite an aggressive demand for the outcomes measured by narrow, standardized testing, classroom teachers might be empowered to reclaim their voices in creating sound pedagogical and content goals and assessments for students, as well as to define the specific knowledge, skills, and dispositions to achieve those goals.

Teachers as disseminators of knowledge

In this metaphor, teaching is viewed as an assembly line in which knowledge is transferred from someone who knows to individuals who do not (Shuell, 1996). Smylie, Bay, and Tozer (1999) argue that most novice teachers define teachers' role as transmitters of knowledge. This role is rooted in the behaviorist-empiricist perspective, which sees knowing as a systematic accumulation of associations and skills. For these associations to happen between stimuli and response, we need a learning process in which various connections and skills are acquired (Floden, 2001). Because teaching happens through transmission of information and skills, this view argues for routinized, sequenced, and well-organized activities so that students will optimize skill learning and acquisition of information. It is important for a teacher to have an explicit plan, including presenting instructional goals, specifying the expectations, procedures, and materials to be learned (Greeno, 1997). This framework is well represented in the instructions for lesson planning in Hunter's (1969) infamous seven-element lesson plans or Gagne's (1965) nine instructional steps. Along the way, it is important to give detailed feedback to students to inform them which component they mastered and which they need to work on through reinforcement and motivation. Michael Apple (1998) describes this model as apparent in standardized curriculum. The notion of teachers being the disseminator of knowledge immediately implies authoritarian and direct teaching practices in order to "place" information into students' minds (Sarason, 1990). This role does not allow space for children to be independent learners and thinkers. This role also does not acknowledge teacher learning when teacher expertise is perceived as perfection in teacher standards as one teacher describes:

> One of the hardest things for me is not to feel ashamed and to try to hide my limitations as a teacher. Part of me believes that in order to be a competent teacher I have to know it all and do it all. Since I don't know very much, it puts a lot of pressure on me to appear to know it all. It has taken the growth of a lot of trust in me to expose my inabilities and to work on them at the same time. (Musanti & Pence, 2010, p. 82)

Teachers as technicians

The role of teachers as "technician" is inspired by cognitive and rationalist perspectives that see knowing as having structures of information and processes that are organized and compartmentalized through schemas and symbols (Floden, 2001). In this frame, the emphasis on experts and curriculum specialists seemingly took some of the responsibility off the shoulders of teachers for the decision of what to and how to teach. Teachers' roles then are reduced to mechanic, technical, and managerial skills to design classroom learning according to the given directions and content goals (Apple, 1998). Apple (1998) argued that although attempts to "professionalize" the teaching profession might add value and prestige to teaching among other more technical and professional occupations and support women in the teaching force to claim a better career level, they also create a loss of creativity and feelings of lockedness and partialness with new divisions of labors for teaching, for example, skill groups, resource room, and compartmentalized subject matter curriculum.

Teachers as facilitators of knowledge construction

In this view, the main responsibility of teachers is to help students construct necessary knowledge and skills to be independent thinkers, to make judgments about their own learning process, and to be responsible and active agents of their own learning (Kennedy, 1999). This view aligns with situative learning theories that emphasize how knowledge is played out in different contexts, communities, and practices through individuals, artifacts, books, materials, social processes, and histories. Vygotsky (1978) defines learning as participation of varying degrees in an activity. Therefore, teaching is achieved by strengthening children's participatory abilities (Greeno, 1997). Teachers facilitate knowledge construction by designing classrooms in a way that allows group learning, inquiry, and social practices of meaning making.

Teaching should support knowledge construction by providing scaffolding for students' learning to move the student to the next level of understanding. One way to apply this knowledge in practice would be to closely observe students to see what they can understand and do without help and then support them so they can reach the next levels of learning in a social learning context (Horowitz, Darling-Hammond, & Bransford, 2005). This scaffolding might take forms such as adjusting the amount and level of help, questioning, demonstrating, bringing students to the edge of their understanding, and deciding when to intervene and when to give space to the learner to problem solve (Rodgers & Rodgers, 2007). To support the development of students' personal identities in a social context, a variety of methods could be used: formulating and evaluating questions, problems, conjectures, arguments, and explanations in a way that will foster and complement differences in social interactions, cultural practices, and expertise (Floden, 2001). To do so, Bransford, Derry, Berliner, Hammerness, and Beckett (2005) argue that it is essential for teachers to help students self-assess their own learning.

Teachers as transformative intellectuals and change agents

If it is important to teach students to be intellectual individuals for a free and democratic society, Henry Giroux (1998), argues, then it is also crucial to see teachers as intellectuals who have transformative potentials. Similarly, Smylie et al. (1999) propose that teachers' role should be change agents in school and in society. Teachers, Giroux proposes, can make this transformation happen only if they can begin questioning about the purposes of schooling and the conditions that shape it, along with questioning why they teach, what they are teaching, and how they are to teach. However, Sarason (1990) argues that sometimes when we load the whole responsibility to "change" the society onto schools and teachers, we are ignoring the fact that society is also shaping schools, teachers, and students at, maybe, deeper levels, so there are limits to what schooling can accomplish. Therefore, during this process, dilemmas and challenges arise; yet teacher educators and administrators should not be hesitant about focusing on the dilemmas and conflicts that teachers have while facing educational change and actually use these as opportunities for reflection, sources of experience and growth, and leadership (Smylie et al., 1999). Therefore, Fullan (1993) argues that change agency has to come together with a moral purpose so that teachers would be willing to take leadership in their schools. This might only happen through a commitment to improve their practices, self-education, and a realization that teaching is life-long learning (Griffin, 1999).

When teachers start to question their role in the classroom and in the greater society, they can begin to critically think about how educational poli-cy and reform efforts interact with their role in the education of students. In the next part, I explore the notion of educational reform as it affects practic-ing teachers and educational change that teachers initiate. I then argue that teachers can address the challenges that current educational reform brings by reclaiming their role in the education of students and in their own profession-al growth.

Educational Reform as It Affects Practicing Teachers

There is no possibility of sustaining school reform without establishing and then building upon a foundation of trust in teachers and in their desire and ability to form life-enhancing relationships with one another and with young people. (Bullough & Kridel, 2003, p. 677)

The phrase *educational reform* carries so many different meanings in the beginning of the 21st century. How does educational change occur and how does this affect practicing teachers? Fullan (2001) describes reform as teach-ers perceive it: "Passing through the zones of uncertainty…the situation of being at sea, of being lost, of confronting more information than you can handle" (p. 31). This is what many teachers feel when top-down approaches of educational reform in the form of new policies, curricular programs, and projects are put into practice each year or with each new federal or state ad-ministration.

Sarason (1990) argues that the main problem with the attempts to reform education has been the failure to notice that schooling is a living system that includes individuals with varying roles to accomplish a common goal instead of a system that is composed of partial perspectives that are seen as adver-saries: "Adversarial attitudes and stands are predictable features of a school system: a mini United Nations in which the pursuit of narrow self-interest is all-pervasive" (p. 25). He admits that administrators who had been in the teachers' positions may arrive at policy decisions and conclusions that are beyond the reality of classrooms because they situate themselves inde-pendently of the classroom context. How do we interpret this from a power dynamics perspective? Educational changes are often planned and created on a policymaker level with minimal support from research, rarely in collaboration with teachers, without considering how teachers would negotiate those with their teaching approaches. Further, adds Michael Apple (1998), although most of the teaching force is composed of women, most of the principals, administrators, and policymakers in education have been upper-class men feeding a *proletarianization* of teaching itself and the teaching force. The dynamics of gender, class, economic, and political issues take part in what is discussed, what needs to be changed, and what counts as success or failure in education.

Indeed, educational change might impact teachers' professional growth, depending on how they perceive it, beyond just influencing the curriculum or teaching methods. Gregoire (2003) explains that teachers perceive change and reform in three levels; benign, challenge, and threat. On the benign level, teachers see the change as very partial and superficial, and they do not consider it as a vehicle for growth. If the change is perceived on the challenge level, teachers are shaken, but they still persist by taking on the challenge in order to learn and develop their knowledge and practice. If they perceive it as a threat, teachers are likely to resist the particular change. Therefore, Gregoire found that because teaching is a highly personal act, content knowledge expertise and pedagogies are important parts of teachers' identity. Therefore, when teachers feel threatened by a change, they seem to respond rather negatively to it. This aligns with findings from other studies reporting that if teachers are more actively involved in the decision making to improve education on the classroom level or on a broader scale, they consider it as challenge; then they might be more willing and active in the process (Richardson & Placier, 2001). When educational change is imposed under the name of regulations and policies and created without collaboration, teachers are more likely to be threatened.

Fullan (2001) argues that the lack of consistent and coherent support for teachers is one factor that makes it harder for teachers to adjust to educational changes. For instance, the most common professional development methods for teachers are brief, one-time workshops at the district level that focus on curriculum and content knowledge. Ironically, the term *workshop* first emerged out of an influential professional development project, the Eight Year Study (1933–1941), whose central concept of teacher education was that "teachers are educated problem solvers" and not mechanics or technicians (Bullough & Kridel, 2003). Yet in teachers' minds, the contemporary notion of professional development often has some negative connotations such as "one-shot workshops," "lecture," or "presentation," most of which are conducted without collaboration and dialogue with the teachers.

Indeed, the link between theory and practice has been a concern for teachers who attend professional development sessions and conferences. These sessions sometimes might be too theoretical, making it hard to translate into classroom teaching. Other times they might be incoherent, inconsistent pieces of prescriptions for a targeted skill without a conceptual base and research support. Finally, they might be part of a top-down educational reform that teachers are bound to learn and apply. With the Obama administration's focus on modifying but not eliminating the road map for NCLB, it seems that preparing teachers for high-stakes testing will continue to be a focus in the professional development of teachers who are "teaching to the test" in this climate of institutional pressure. This has dramatic implications for how teachers think about the teaching and learning process. Boardman and Woodruff (2004) found that teachers in their study became more willing to adopt innovative teaching techniques if they believed that these techniques might be utilized for the purpose of preparing students for the testing. Then how can teacher educators, administrators, and policymakers support teachers to have valuable experiences, practices, and meaningful learning through professional development that also respond to their day-to-day struggles?

Bullough and Kridel (2003) argue that the professional development of teachers should actively engage teachers in the process of learning through cooperative efforts and sustaining engagement through particular tasks and problems in order to connect theoretical ideas and practical implications. Professional development should not be divorced from daily concerns, regarded as the responsibility of administrators alone, and considered as compartmentalized or mechanical. Instead, it should offer knowledge relevant to teachers' lives, consider teacher qualities and strengths as a beginning point, and focus on the analysis of research and daily practices (Shields, Bishop, & Mazawi, 2005). Indeed, long-term practices of professional development that take teachers' personal experiences into consideration and foster self-understanding and collaboration among teachers have strengthened teachers' beliefs about their competency in teaching all children (Rosenfeld & Rosenfeld, 2008). Such a perspective helps us understand why the professional development sessions on "change" have often faced resistance from teachers as it implied that something was inherently wrong or lacking in their teaching (Apple, 1998).

Now it is time to look at the Obama administration's vision for structuring how teachers learn, develop, and gain expertise and how we can support teachers in the process:

> But even though we know how much teaching matters, in too many places we've abandoned our teachers, sending them into some of the most impoverished, under-performing schools with little experience or pay; little preparation or support. After a few years of experience, most will leave to pick wealthier, less challenging schools.
>
> The result is that some of our neediest children end up with less-experienced, poorly-paid teachers who are far more likely to be teaching subjects in which they have no training. Minority students are twice as likely to have these teachers. In Illinois, students in high-poverty schools are more than three times as likely to have them. The No Child Left Behind law, which states that all kids should have highly qualified teachers, is supposed to correct this, but so far it hasn't, because no one's followed through on the promise. (Obama, 2005)

When we look at this speech that President Obama delivered seven years ago, we can see that teachers are classified into two categories: ones who are highly qualified and ones who are doing a poor job, partly because they lack experience. However, it is not sufficient to create simple dichotomies without considering the long process of teacher growth. After all, the notion of "highly qualified teachers" is an essentialist but still subjective construct and one we as educators strive to achieve by providing teachers opportunities for growth over the years. Teacher growth does not happen in a vacuum or overnight. Labeling teachers as highly qualified or not will only escalate the pressure that all teachers feel when their students do not score high on the tests regardless of how much they supported their students' knowledge and skills and social and emotional growth. Nevertheless, when we look at these dichotomies by which teachers are classified, the need for providing professional education opportunities for practicing teachers seems obvious, especially the kind of professional development that is teacher initiated and supports teacher growth, instead of marginalizing the ones that are "doing a poor job."

Elsewhere, President Obama discusses some of the responses to "failing" schools that make teachers the objects of reform discourses. Teacher voices are still not heard, and they are subject to change without being subjects of it:

> You know the arguments. On one side, you'll hear conservatives who will look at children without textbooks and classrooms without computers and say money

doesn't matter. On the other side, you'll find liberals who will look at failing test scores and failing schools and not realize how much reform matters. One side will blame teachers, and the other side will never ask them to change. Some will say that no matter what you do, some children just can't learn. Others will make excuses for them when they won't learn. (Obama, 2005)

I call for a pair of fresh lenses so that we can perceive who the teachers are and can be. Teachers cannot be reduced to objects of policy debates. At the core of the issues is a danger: When we try to understand the issues with schooling and look at teachers from the outside, we might fall into the trap of seeing teaching as any other occupation, an occupation in which competitiveness and business world principles rule. In other words, as we continue to see teachers as technicians (Sleeter, 2008) and employees and not intellectuals or facilitators of learning, we are inclined to impose strategies such as competitive grants or incentives for successful teachers and force others who are less successful into leaving the profession per market rules. However, in the next section, I suggest a change in our thinking, a change in how we perceive teachers. We need to acknowledge teachers as capable of producing professional knowledge about the teaching and learning process. Therefore, in this climate of increased accountability without prerogative or entitlement to their profession, teachers need support and encouragement that is oriented in their local learning communities more than financial incentives or threats to engage in a professional learning process in their local schools.

Teachers as Producers of Professional Knowledge

In this section, I discuss some of the current practices of professional education for teachers oriented in teacher knowledge and practices. I also seek answers to the question: How can we describe educational change that teachers could initiate even in this era of high-stakes testing and teacher accountability so they can reclaim their active role in the teaching and learning process? One response to this question is that as teachers reclaim their voices for their own growth, they could utilize the concept of *professional knowledge*. Professional knowledge is defined "as insights and understandings that teachers develop themselves, besides the general knowledge that is generated for teachers by others" (Ponte, Ax, Beijaard, & Wubbels, 2004, p. 571). Thus, teacher knowledge not only includes content knowledge and teaching strategies, it also involves many other layers that teachers construct through practicing their profession (Ponte et al., 2004). Smylie et al. (1999) argue that professional knowledge needs to be an amalgam of formal theories, empirical research, and careful analysis and critique of experiences in teaching and learning. Professional knowledge could be utilized as a productive tool in teachers' professional growth and even a means that teachers use to create small-scale educational changes above and beyond imposed reforms or standardized expectations or benchmarks for growth. As we reclaim the active role of teachers in their own professional learning process as well as K-12 student learning, it is important to support teachers and provide them with the tools for sound educational change in their classrooms, buildings, and districts. Here, I identify three outlets through which practicing teachers could create professional knowledge that represents the realities of their local context and which are appropriate for their and their students' needs: reflective practices, practitioner research, and inquiry communities. As I describe each of these, I give examples of research with teachers that reflect how these outlets can support teachers in their endeavor of guiding teaching and learning processes.

Reflective Practices

Zeichner (2005) sees reflective practices as a vital part in the supervision and support of new teachers. He asserts that to be able to support the process of learning to teach, conversations that make teachers' thinking process and reasoning over their particular choices are crucial. Gregoire (2003) agrees that the opportunity for reflection is necessary for any professional development program. He also urges policymakers that teachers should be given the opportunity to collaboratively reflect and think about the possible implications of reforms on their existing classroom practices. However, policies and new implementations change each year and demand immediate results on the classroom teaching and student learning (Boardman & Woodruff, 2004). For instance, the urge to demonstrate instant success with testing not only leaves little time for reflection but also encourages teachers to focus on the quick products and scores. Reflective practices support classroom teaching and student learning in many ways that are meaningful to teachers. These practices might help teachers understand their own way of learning and thinking, in turn supporting their understanding of where students are, how they think and learn, and how thinking processes of students and teachers differ (Sarason, 1990) so that teachers can better support students' learning. One of the examples of how teacher educators encourage teachers to reflect on their practices is through the use of metaphors. Stofflett (1996) encouraged class-room teachers to develop metaphors that represent the way they see teaching and learning. The study reportedly benefited teachers who did not realize what kinds of experiences influence them to develop metaphors such as sav-ior, gardener, and coach and how these shape their expectations from stu-dents and the pedagogies they utilize. In another study, university educators (Brown, Castle, Rogers, Feuerhelm, & Chimblo, 2007) observed Kay, the second-grade teacher, as she practiced reflection through journaling and ana-lyzing daily teaching:

> Maybe I need to make the discussion point related to an activity where everybody was very actively involved, rather than just about a book. Maybe we could do an ac-tivity where we pretend to be on a bus, but not everybody gets to sit on the front of the bus...like Rosa Parks. My class keeps bringing her name up when we have these discussions. They relate to the fact that she stood up for what she knew was right. (p. 10)

Fullan (2001) states that reflective practices also influence how teachers think about educational change. When teachers question their previously held beliefs and change their habits, this would lead to *reculturation*. Recultura-tion allows more substantial changes than *restructuring* does, which happens when teachers try to adopt new strategies on a superficial level without think-ing deeply about its meaning or why it might be needed. Therefore, as Bullough and Baughman (1997) argue, positive change in beliefs and com-mitments requires long-term dialogue, participation, and a sustained effort by both teachers and teacher educators. In a recent study, a preservice teacher in a challenging inner-city classroom reflected on her learning process when the team of three teachers discovered that the classroom issues indicated a lack of community, and change was needed to create a positive classroom envi-ronment for student learning:

> What I am learning from this experience is it is all about building the community here. We came at the end of the year, we have already at least 6-7 kids that don't like each other. When I split them up in pairs, (they say) "I don't want to work with this person." I would stress that (at the) beginning of the year. That building that family, community. That is what I would do that would make it different. (Katz & Isik-Ercan, 2009)

Practitioner Research

Practitioner research is a relatively new term and might imply that teachers are just recently starting to engage in systematic inquiry into the teaching and learning process. However, Henson (1996) argues that since the early 20th century, teachers have been involved in research projects, although in subordinate roles, such as collecting data and helping researchers backstage sometimes without even learning the results. Yet research can be most beneficial to the teachers if they conduct the studies independently or at least with an equal collaboration partnership. As many school districts increasingly value research-based strategies, methods, or teaching techniques, teachers may take roles in piloting, assessing, and researching new practices before they are put into effect (Henson, 1996). A first-year teacher describes how she used the results of her action study:

> I used action research just to grow professionally….As I look back at things I did…I don't agree with some of the things I tried just knowing there are other things I could have done, but it did help me grow in the other way to say what I won't do again. (Gilles, Wilson, & Elias, 2010, p. 102)

Lieberman and Miller (2001) suggest that practitioner inquiry could be an outlet for teachers who are in search of professional growth beyond the question of "what works": Powerful teacher education is more than a matter of learning about and practicing a set of promising teaching techniques but, instead, of engagement in the exploration, with others, of problems and issues of pressing personal and professional concern, the sort of issues that are now the focus of growing teacher researcher movement. (Bullough & Kridel, 2003, p. 677)

Yet as Ponte et al. (2004) found, many practitioner research studies have been aimed only to improve teachers' technological knowledge, which is mainly about strategies, techniques, and practices for a certain activity. Simply focusing on what works or not limits the potential of practitioner inquiry as a means for professional development. Systematic research is needed to explore other ways that practitioner inquiry could be utilized for teachers' professional growth, still in connection to their everyday practices: "Undertaking research focused on the practical teaching decisions that swirl around teachers daily allows them to take a self-regulated and powerful stance toward their teaching lives" (Meier & Henderson, 2007, p. 8). As an example,

Ponte et al. (2004) explored how practitioner research might facilitate teachers in developing professional knowledge. The authors suggest that the higher levels of knowledge such as ideological or empirical knowledge could be developed with the support of university educators. As indicated in the Ponte et al. (2004) study, collaboration between teacher educators and teachers is important in achieving teacher goals that are classified as professional, pedagogical, intellectual, and personal. University researchers could support this process by helping teachers understand that theories, research epistemologies and methodologies could be tools for thinking deeply about issues surrounding schooling (Jungck, 2001). Ponte et al. (2004) found that the university-based facilitators of practitioner research have been most helpful when they only offered insights, suggestions, and feedback during the actual research process that teachers led. This way it implies a closer connection between teacher educators and school sites to enhance their knowledge and practices.

Inquiry Communities

Teacher isolation is an interesting dilemma for teachers, Fullan (2001) argues. It is a dilemma because there are two sides of the coin: On one side, teachers often lack productive adult interactions and dialogues throughout the day, and teaching remains a private act behind closed doors for the most part of the school day (Smylie, Bay, & Tozer, 1999; Sarason, 1990). On the other side, it is challenging for teachers to undertake collegiality as a means for growth and support. Even experienced teachers might have difficulty in seeing teacher interactions and working together as sustaining support and professional experience for themselves. It takes time to build trust, Robb (2000) notes. However, for teachers who begin an inquiry process into their teaching, the need to exchange ideas and engage in professional conversations with peers might be inspiring and rewarding (Hobson, 2001). Stodolsky and Grossman (2000) point to the vital role of cultural and structural transformation on the school community. The myth of a hero teacher who alone can create any kinds of change and overcome all challenges no longer exists. Therefore, one of the purposes of inquiry communities should be to create opportunities for teachers to work together with one another and negotiate their understandings on professional learning. When diverse groups of experienced teachers, who bring different knowledge and experiences, form communities of plural discourses, the insights and discussions might be very rich (Putnam & Borko, 2000). A high school teacher describes how profound an inquiry community can become in supporting teachers:

> For me, collaboration is more…it involves talk about beliefs, understandings, values, a shared language develops…involves sharing a purpose and finding support and understanding when issues and dilemmas arise. Respect, trust, and the preservation of individual integrity are also important aspects of collaboration. I have a true and heart-felt feeling of collaboration with the teachers in the learning community. We have a common, explicit purpose; we talk often about beliefs, values, and understandings. In fact, they drive everything we do. We respect and trust one another; we value individual perspectives, and feel comfortable disagreeing and arguing. (Rose, 1999, pp. 62–63)

Griffin (1999) elaborates that a collegial and collaborative support system will engage prospective, novice, and experienced teachers in an effort to transform teaching from an isolated activity into a foundation for school success. This way inquiry communities could support teachers to build a positive classroom and school culture. Professional conversations around inquiry communities might also lead to positive experiences with educational change if teachers are encouraged to discuss these and analyze changes to interpret the local meaning of a particular reform. By doing this, teachers will be reculturing and creating true learning communities (Fullan, 2001).

Can induction and mentoring programs be utilized as part of inquiry communities for new teachers to undertake challenges? Smith and Ingersoll (2004) found that mentoring programs create effective results when new teachers have a mentor from the same expertise area, when they have common planning time with other teachers, and when they have opportunities for collaboration and conversations on their teaching. Teachers are less likely to leave the teaching field with the support of a network of teachers. These research findings are also supported by Fullan (2001), who concludes that a professionally rewarding workplace designed to energize teachers in a community climate should be a first step to reverse the deterioration of the conditions of the work teachers have to undertake. Therefore, inquiry communities as an overlooked factor in teacher retention should be seriously considered in the Obama administration in order to increase teacher quality.

Implications and Recommendations for Policy

This chapter addresses two groups of people: teachers, who are the meaning makers of teaching and learning, and policymakers, who are interpreting this process from an administrative and supervisory point.

The Obama administration should consider that becoming a "qualified and effective" teacher is an endeavor that lasts throughout one's career. Thus, initial preparation of teachers and supporting them as they continue their practice are equally important. However, at the center of the initiations for change need to be teachers' voices that seem lost in policy discussions of today. Especially in the new realm of quick alternative routes to teacher certification that produces teachers without much practice in teaching and field experiences, it is apparent that multiple ways to provide professional development for practicing teachers will be in such demand that the federal administration will need to rethink and refocus on teacher learning during teaching practice. Only in this way can we move away from simplistic dichotomies about "effective" and noneffective teachers and see the complexity of the teaching and learning process in various contexts.

I argued in this chapter that by understanding the ways their roles are historically, socially, and politically shaped, teachers might reclaim their voices in the teaching and learning process. The three outlets I suggested for professional development allow teachers' voices to be heard loud and clear in the teaching and learning process. The Obama administration should support any local and contextual efforts of teachers to engage in these kinds of meaningful learning practices. Instead of offering competitions for fewer teacher development grants, each school or district should be expected to submit a local professional development plan that is funded in moderate amounts. Outcomes for such professional development efforts should be evaluated through multiple measures, including reports, samples of successful practices, teacher and student artifacts, in addition to standardized tests and surveys, and these assessments must also reflect teachers' ideas and suggestions for change.

Multiple influences on teaching and learning should be considered before any assumptions of teaching effectiveness could be made. The Obama administration should value efforts advocating for multiple measures of teaching effectiveness and move away from interpreting teacher effectiveness through single measures such as high-stakes testing. Listening to teacher voices is important in the process of revising current practices of accountability. For instance, through a survey of 708 teachers, Jones and Egley (2004) found that teachers did not oppose the notion of accountability through assessments, yet they objected to the way it is implemented as the true indicator of student learning and teacher quality. They thought that one-time test scores are not an accurate assessment of students' learning and development, and when used this way, such assessment resulted in decreased student and teacher motivation. The Obama administration should reconceptualize education as the culmination of activities supporting physical, socioemotional, and cognitive growth and consider assessment systems that measure capabilities and potentials beyond comprehending factual information on subject matter. This way, teachers will not be reduced to "technicians" or "disseminators of knowledge."

Conclusion

Admittedly, calling for teacher voices is becoming harder for teacher educators in the midst of harsh policy discourses pointed at higher education institutions that traditionally produce intellectual property and do not have monetary or status-based powers. Although teacher education institutions underwent a transformation and growth during the last decades, it is unclear whether policymakers are up to date with successful and effective practices to educate teacher candidates through exemplary teacher education programs during preservice teacher education. One of the most important findings from the current research is that rigorous field experiences and clinical practices strongly support teachers in their first few years and help provide a sense of confidence and perseverance in the profession (Darling-Hammond, 2006). However, institutions for teacher preparation still seem to be left out of policy discussions along with the teachers.

Second, the core goal of teacher learning and development since the report *A Nation at Risk* (National Commission on Excellence in Education, 1983) was published, has been the vague concept of teacher "quality" and "effectiveness," with inevitable linking of this concept to student learning and achievement in this era of standardized testing and increased accountability of teachers. Typically, programs designed for teacher learning include workshops and generic training that do not reflect the contexts and local communities that teachers are engaged in and, thus, are rarely regarded as valuable by teachers. Recently, there are calls for reconsidering avenues of professional development to focus on teacher learning.

In this chapter, I proposed three avenues that orient teachers in learning: reflective practices, practitioner research, and inquiry communities. Wenger's (1999) social theory of learning explains how learning has multiple dimensions such as "learning as doing (practice)," "learning as belonging (community)," "learning as experience (meaning)," and "learning as becoming (identity)." Moreover, Wenger (1999) argues that learning processes always occur at the social realm. The three avenues I describe clearly encompass these four dimensions of teacher learning and correspond to Wenger's (1999) notion of "communities of practice" because these avenues consider teacher learning in its complexity beyond measuring student test scores on math and language arts. Only when teachers are supported to reflect on their own practices can they act on this new learning, engage in systematic inquiries into their teaching and student learning, and professionally connect to their colleagues on classroom, department, school, community, district, regional, and national levels. Therefore, although they cannot overcome institutional challenges, teachers can still reclaim their voices on several levels by engaging in reflective practices and practitioner inquiry in a community of learners so that they can be true influences in their students' lives. In her poignant book, *Teacher as Stranger*, Maxine Greene (1973) calls for these teacher voices:

> We simply suggest that he struggle against unthinking submerge in the social reality that prevails. If he wishes to present himself as a person actively engaged in critical thinking and authentic choosing, he cannot accept any "ready-made standardized scheme" at face value. He cannot even take for granted the value of intelligence, rationality, or education. Why, after all, *should* a human being act intelligently or rationally? How does a teacher justify the educational policies he is assigned to carry out within his school? If the teacher does not pose such questions to himself, he cannot expect his students to pose the kinds of questions about experience which will not involve them in self-aware inquiry. (p. 269)

References

Apple, M. (1998). Controlling the work of teachers. In H. S. Shapiro & D. E. Purpel (Eds.), *Critical social issues in American education* (pp. 255–271). New York: Longman.

Boardman, A. G., & Woodruff, A. L. (2004). Teacher change and "high stakes" assessment: What happens to professional development? *Teaching and Teacher Education, 20,* 545–557.

Bransford, J., Derry, S., Berliner, D., Hammerness, K., & Beckett, K. L. (2005). Theories of learning and their roles in teaching. In L. Darling-Hammond & J. Bransford (Eds.), *Preparing teachers for a changing world* (pp. 40–87). San Francisco, CA: Jossey-Bass.

Brown, P., Castle, K., Rogers, K. M., Feuerhelm, C., & Chimblo, S. (2007). The nature of primary teaching: Body, time, space, and relationships. *Journal of Early Childhood Teacher Education, 28,* 3–16.

Bullough, R. V., & Baughman, K. (1997). *First-year teacher eight years later: An inquiry into teacher development.* New York: Teachers College Press.

Bullough, R. V., & Kridel, C. (2003). Workshops, inservice education, and the Eight Year Study. *Teaching and Teacher Education, 19,* 665–679.

Darling-Hammond, L. (2006). *Powerful teacher education: Lessons from exemplary programs.* San Francisco, CA: Jossey-Bass.

Floden, R. E. (2001). Research on effects of teaching: A continuing model for research on teaching. In V. Richardson (Ed.), *Handbook of research on teaching* (4th ed., pp. 3–16). Washington, DC: American Educational Research Association.

Fullan, M. (1993). Why teachers must become change agents. *Educational Leadership, 50,* 12–17.

———. (2001). *The new meaning of educational change.* New York: Teachers College Press.

Gagne, R. M. (1965). *The conditions of learning.* New York: Rinehart and Winston.

Gilles, C., Wilson, J., & Elias, M. (2010). Sustaining teachers' growth and renewal through action research, induction programs, and collaboration. *Teacher Education Quarterly, 37*(1), 91–108.

Giroux, H. A. (1998). Teacher as transformative intellectuals. In H. S. Shapiro & D. E. Purpel (Eds.), *Critical social issues in American education* (pp. 255–271). New York: Longman.

Greene, M. (1973). *Teacher as stranger: Educational philosophy for the modern age.* Belmont, CA: Wadsworth.

Greeno, J. (1997). Theories and practices of thinking and learning to think. *American Journal of Education, 106,* 85–126.

Gregoire, M. (2003). Is it a challenge or a threat? A dual process model of teachers' cognition and appraisal processes during conceptual change. *Educational Psychology Review, 15,* 147–179.

Griffin, G. A. (1999). Changes in teacher education: Looking to the future. In G. Griffin (Ed.), *The education of teachers* (pp. 20–28). Part 1, 98th Yearbook of the National Society for the Study of Education. Chicago: National Society for the Study of Education.

Henson, K. T. (1996). Teachers as researchers. In J. Sikula (Ed.), *Handbook of research on teacher education* (2nd ed., pp. 53–64). New York: Macmillan.

Hobson, D. (2001). Learning with each other: Collaboration in teacher research. In G. Burnaford, J. Fischer, & D. Hobson (Eds.), *Teachers doing research: The power of action through inquiry* (4th ed., pp. 173–191). Mahwah, NJ: Lawrence Erlbaum Associates.

Horowitz, F. D., Darling-Hammond, L., & Bransford, J. (2005). Educating teachers for developmentally appropriate practice. In L. Darling-Hammond & J. Bransford (Eds.), *Preparing teachers for a changing world* (pp. 88–125). San Francisco, CA: Jossey-Bass.

Hunter, M. (1969). *Improved instruction.* Thousands Oaks, CA: Corwin Press.

Jalongo, M. R., & Isenberg, J. P. (1995). *Professional development. Teachers' stories: From personal narrative to professional insight.* San Francisco, CA: Jossey-Bass.

Jones, B. D., & Egley, R. J. (2004). Voices from the frontlines: Teachers' perceptions of high-stakes testing. *Educational Policy Analysis Archives, 12*(39), 1–29.

Jungck, S. (2001). How does it matter? Teacher inquiry in the traditions of social science research. In G. Burnaford, J. Fischer, & D. Hobson (Eds.), *Teachers doing research: The power of action through inquiry* (2nd ed., pp. 329–343). Mahwah, NJ: Lawrence Erlbaum Associates.

Katz, L., & Isik-Ercan, Z. (2009, April). *Reconceptualizing field experiences and its relationship to other teacher preparation contexts.* Paper presented at the annual meeting of American Educational Research Association, San Diego, CA.

Kennedy, M. M. (1999). The role of preservice teacher education. In L. Darling-Hammond & G. Sykes (Eds.), *Teaching as the learning profession: Handbook of policy and practice* (pp. 54–85). San Francisco, CA: Jossey-Bass.

Kumashiro, K. K. (2010). Seeing the bigger picture: Troubling movements to end teacher education. *Journal of Teacher Education, 61*(1–2), 56–65.

Lieberman, A., & Miller, L. (2001). Introduction. In A. Lieberman & L. Miller (Eds.), *Teachers caught in action: Professional development that matters* (pp. vii–x). New York: Teachers College Press.

Meier, D. R., & Henderson, B. (2007). *Learning from young children in the classroom: The art and science of teacher research.* New York: Teachers College Press.

Musanti, S. I., & Pence, L. (2010). Collaboration and teacher development: Unpacking resistance, constructing knowledge, and navigating identities. *Teacher Education Quarterly, 37*(1), 73–89.

National Commission on Excellence in Education. (1983). *A nation at risk: The imperative for educational reform.* Washington, DC: Author.

Obama, B. H. (2010). *Remarks by the president at the America's Promise Alliance Education event.* Retrieved March 20, 2010, from http://www.whitehouse.gov/the-press-office/remarks-president-americas-promise-alliance-education-event.

————. (2005, October 25). *Teaching our kids in a 21st century economy*. Speech delivered to the Center for American Progress. Retrieved December 21, 2008, from http://www. barackobama.com/2005/10/25/teaching_our_kids_in_a_21st_ce.php

Organizing for America. (2008). *Solution for education*. Retrieved June 23, 2010, from http:// www.barackobama.com/issues/education/

Ponte, P., Ax, J., Beijaard, D., & Wubbels, T. (2004). Teachers' development of professional knowledge through action research and the facilitation of this by teacher educators. *Teaching and Teacher Education, 20*, 571–588.

Putnam, R., & Borko, H. (2000). What do new views of knowledge and thinking have to say about research on teacher learning? *Educational Researcher, 29*(1), 4–15.

Richardson, V., & Placier, P. (2001). Teacher change. In V. Richardson (Ed.), *Handbook of research on teaching* (4th ed., pp. 905–947). Washington, DC: American Educational Research Association.

Robb, L. (2000). *Redefining staff development: A collaborative model for teachers and administrators*. Portsmouth, NH: Heinemann.

Rodgers, A., & Rodgers E. (2007). *The effective literacy coach*. New York: Teachers College Press.

Rose, C. (1999). Shaping Sara's practice. In F. M. Connelly & D. J. Clandinin (Eds.), *Shaping a professional identity: Stories of educational practice* (pp. 42–63). New York: Teachers College Press.

Rosenfeld, M., & Rosenfeld, S. (2008). Developing effective teacher beliefs about learners: The role of sensitizing teachers to individual learning differences. *Educational Psychology, 28*(3), 245–272.

Sarason, S. B. (1990). *The predictable failure of educational reform*. San Francisco, CA: Jossey-Bass.

Shields, C. M., Bishop, R., & Mazawi, A. E. (2005). *Pathologizing practices: The impact of deficit thinking in education*. New York: Peter Lang.

Shuell, T. (1996). Teaching and learning in classroom contexts. In D. Berliner & R. Calfee (Eds.), *Handbook of educational psychology* (pp. 726–764). New York: Macmillan.

Sleeter, C. (2008). Equity, democracy, and neoliberal assaults on teacher education. *Teaching and Teacher Education, 24*(8), 1947–1952.

Smith, T. M., & Ingersoll, R. M. (2004). What are the effects of induction and mentoring on beginning teacher turnover? *American Educational Research Journal, 41*(3), 681–714.

Smylie, M., Bay, M., & Tozer, S. (1999). Preparing teachers as agents of change. In G. Griffin (Ed.), *The education of teachers* (pp. 29–62). Part 1, 98th Yearbook of the National Society for the Study of Education. Chicago: National Society for the Study of Education.

Stodolsky, S. S., & Grossman, P. L. (2000). Changing students, changing teachers. *Teachers College Record, 102*, 125–172.

Stofflett, R. T. (1996). Metaphor development by secondary teachers enrolled in graduate teacher education. *Teaching and Teacher Education, 12*(6), 577–589.

Vygotsky, L. S. (1978). *Mind in society: The development of higher psychological processes.* Cambridge, MA: Harvard University Press.

Wenger, E. (1999). *Communities of practice: Learning, meaning and identity.* Cambridge, UK: Cambridge University Press.

Zeichner, K. (2005). Becoming a teacher educator: A personal perspective. *Teaching and Teacher Education, 21,* 117–124.

CHAPTER FIVE

Teacher Collaborations Provide an Opportunity to Improve Education for All Students Along the Continuum of Learning

Jane M. Leatherman, Nancy J. Bangel,
Tracy L. Cox, Amber Merrill, & Rebecca D. Newsome

Ryan (all student names are pseudonyms) entered my second-grade classroom without knowing his alphabet, let alone being able to read at the same level as his classmates. He left my class at the end of the year reading at a beginning second-grade level. He had advanced more than 2 years in his reading ability—and the current system of accountability labeled him as a failure!

Matt is taking English I again because he did not pass the English I test. Matt started the semester on a second-grade reading level and ended up on a fifth-grade reading level. But according to the English test, he is still not up to grade level even though he made huge progress during that semester. He should be graded according to his growth and improvement.

Ryan, a student in Ms. Cox's class, and Matt, a student in Ms. Newsome's class, are not alone—there are many children who are moving forward but have not reached that arbitrary, magical level of readiness deemed "normal" for their age. There are also many others who have the ability to move beyond this prescribed readiness level but are not given the chance because they have met the required goal and provide no incentive to the school for advancement. With the current accountability system, the school gains nothing by moving children beyond the predetermined basic levels typically based on state standards.

In *The Audacity of Hope*, President Obama (2006) outlined his beliefs concerning the education of America's children. Those beliefs included a need for an economic consensus that would provide an investment in education, a joint responsibility between the school and the children's parents, and a belief that providing money for programs and "the way public schools are managed" (p. 191) by government matters. The argument was made that "America's schools are not holding up their end of the bargain" (p. 189) that if you work hard, you will have a chance for a better life. President Obama noted many of the problems plaguing our schools—the common occurrence of low-quality inner-city schools, high dropout rates, low math and science scores, and a lack of preparation for college-level classes—and he decried the American "tolerance for mediocrity" (p. 190). How are these beliefs going to be translated into practices that will benefit the Ryans and Matts of this world as well as their high-ability classmates? As we struggle to change the perceived as well as real problems in our schools, what changes need to be made and where?

School administrations as well as legislators, the parties holding the purse strings and the power over schools, often declare that they are doing all that is right and good for students. School mission statements almost universally declare, in one form or another, that the school provides a caring, nurturing, and stimulating environment that enables *all* students to reach their full potential. For their part, federal, state, and local legislators implement policies that they believe will hold all public schools accountable for achieving the same goal. Most recently, in *A Blueprint for Reform: The Reauthorization of the Elementary and Secondary Education Act* (hereafter referred to as the *Blueprint*) (U.S. Department of Education, 2010), President Obama asserts that many countries are out-educating us. He states that we must "raise the expectations for our students, for our schools, and for ourselves." He proposes that we do so by making sure that all students are college- and career-ready when they graduate from high school. In his introduction to the *Blueprint* (U.S. Department of Education, 2010), President Obama maintains, "We must foster school environments where teachers have the time to collaborate, the opportunities to lead, and the respect that all professionals deserve." However, with current trends in educational policy, we question how committed policymakers are to making these defensible goals to result in benefits for all students.

The voices offered in this chapter are of those who live daily with the ramifications created by current legislation. These voices of teachers, administrators, and teacher educators illustrate the difficulties and indifference experienced daily by students and teachers. The voices also share possible solu-solutions, most importantly being given the time and resources to collaborate in order to meet the accountability goals while also meeting the needs of all students in the inclusive general education classroom. These teachers and administrators emphasize that general education teachers skilled in grade-level curriculum and standards need the opportunity to collaborate with other educators who are skilled in meeting the distinctive needs of students at both ends of the spectrum in order to meet all of their students' needs.

Needs of Special Education and High-Ability Students

It is our belief that current accountability measures have created an atmosphere that does not allow for resources to be used to enable students with special needs, *struggling or high ability*, to have their unique needs addressed or met. The very legislation that has been created to protect our most valuable resources, our children, has created a system that results in teachers not being allowed to do the very job for which they are trained—to truly meet the needs of all students in their classes. Special education and high-ability students are subjected to a curriculum and standards that, by their very nature, were not intended to meet the needs of struggling or gifted students.

For example, it is noted in the Indiana third-grade mathematics standards, under Number Sense, that third-grade students should be able to "count, read, and write whole numbers up to 1,000" (Indiana State Board of Education, 2000, p. 25). They also learn to order and round numbers up to 1,000, develop the concept of equivalent fractions, and begin to develop the concept of decimals. Curriculum and assessments are then written to ensure that students in the inclusive third-grade classroom can perform these functions.

However, look into the classroom and consider the children who are having difficulty understanding place value; ones, tens, thousands; let alone decimal places. The standards declare they should be competent in these concepts; all the work they encounter in their classroom expresses these concepts in one fashion or another; their classmates seem to understand. They are labeled "failures" because they cannot understand. These struggling students are the ones who need to have the information presented in a different format or at a different conceptual level in order to understand. They may need to see and manipulate the concepts of place value before they are able to be assessed on its merits. Students with special learning differences may need to be exposed to the concepts multiple times before it really becomes a known fact for them. On the opposite end of the spectrum is the child who has understood numbers since he was 4 years old. He can add, subtract, multiply, and divide numbers with much larger values, but he also experiences the same work as the child who is struggling. How does the classroom teacher balance the need to develop curriculum based on academic standards with the reality that these standards do not fit many of his or her students? Can assistance be garnered through collaboration with educators specially trained to adjust this curriculum to the unique needs of individual students?

To what do we refer when we speak of the unique needs of struggling and high-ability students? It is much easier to note that these students have unique needs than it is to conceptualize these needs. *Struggling students* is a term used to identify such a vastly diverse group of students who have needs that are as unique as they are that to generalize their needs would be futile. However, they all need teachers who understand their individual uniqueness and teachers who know how to address these unique needs. When we speak of children who struggle academically, the label tells us nothing of the individual child. We need to examine why the child is struggling and what is causing him to stumble and fall. This takes an instructor who has special insights into the difficulties the child is experiencing. Without advanced training, general classroom teachers do not have the specialized training to provide the needed insights to address the individual student's needs.

High-ability students often have their own unique needs generated by a set of common characteristics. These include having a large bank of information on which to draw as well as quick mastery and recall of this and new information. In addition, they frequently grasp underlying principles of new concepts and understand material that is generally at a higher level of complexity than their age peers. These characteristics again lead to a need for teachers who understand their needs and are willing and able to provide learning experiences that are presented at a faster pace and more complex level than for the average learner. As a second-grade teacher put it, "I think the high-ability kids are more challenging than the lower ability. It is easier to see, if they don't get it, we have to re-teach it. It is real easy to overlook the kids who got it; I am pushing them to the side."

As with many students who exhibit strong creative and critical thinking abilities, high-ability students need activities that are not often presented in today's test-driven environment to develop these abilities. Additionally, struggling students may need a different presentation or format of lesson to fully understand the standard. Unfortunately, in our current "drill-and-kill" test preparation, there is little need or opportunity to provide adequately paced and complex instruction. It is interesting to note that President Obama stated, "If we want an innovation economy, one that generates more Googles each year, then we have to invest in our future innovators" (Obama, 2006, p. 197). How do we "invest in our future" when teaching to meet minimum standards sets the bar?

Although it is common to identify struggling students, not all schools have formal systems or procedures for identifying and challenging high-ability students. This often results in a lack of accommodations being provided for these students. In other situations, as noted by the principal from a small rural school, "We just formally started an identification process with our high-ability students....Teachers are working on formal lesson plans for high-ability students. *However, not every teacher gets to participate in that process, so collaboration time would be ideal to discuss those lessons and then the students will benefit.*"

Before you begin to think in terms of students being labeled as struggling, average, or high ability, let us remember that students do not fit into any one neatly labeled and predesigned area but can fall anywhere along a wide continuum of learning. In addition, students most often succeed at varying levels along the continuum in different content areas. One who struggles in mathematics may be quite talented when working in the language arts. To complicate things further, students are often twice exceptional; they may have a learning disability while being among the most highly able. Their achievement test scores often do not give a true indication of their abilities when their disability interferes with their performance. In addition, this leads to a tendency to identify them by their deficiencies as reinforced by their test scores while ignoring their strengths.

The prescribed test, curriculum, and standards do not allow for the needed flexibility for the general education classroom teacher to meet the diverse needs of his or her students. The priority of the current educational system lies in preparing students for the test, and teachers are required to demonstrate that they are teaching to the test and standards. How individual students meet the requirements of these tests is not important nor is their learning. Teachers need assistance to be able to meet the expectations concerning the standardized tests while meeting their professional goals, those of advancing their students' knowledge and learning. From where will this assistance come?

The trained teacher looks for the answers and hopes to be permitted to help the struggling and advanced student. Unfortunately, time and resources are not available to differentiate for each of these students. We must follow one path; we must provide "equal" (translated into "same") opportunities for all students. Although the standards are written for the "average" student, the struggling student is expected to meet this same standard by virtue of his or her age, not ability. And the child who could count to 1,000 when he was 4 years old? At age 9, he is only required to be able to count to 1,000 to meet the standard, the accountability measure. There is no advantage to moving him forward—he has met our requirement. Teaching is a *profession*, not a prescribed curriculum to be followed.

In *The Audacity of Hope* (Obama, 2006), it was declared that "too many of our schools depend on inexperienced teachers with little training in the subjects they're teaching" (p. 191). There is so much emphasis today on teachers having "content knowledge" that we forget that the "how" of teaching is every bit as important a "subject" as the "what." Many people are quite knowledgeable in their field, whether it be technology, medicine, auto mechanics, and so on, but they would not have the content knowledge of the individual needs of the diverse body we call a classroom of students. President Obama (2006) argued that, "by the end of two years, most [young people interested in teaching, predominantly referring to Teach for America trained educators] have either changed careers or moved to suburban schools—a consequence of low pay, a lack of support from the educational bureaucracy, and a pervasive feeling of isolation" (p. 192). We offer the counterargument that they leave the field at the end of their contract because they have found that the content knowledge gained in their training prior to education was insufficient to understand the larger picture of teaching. They often have adequate knowledge of content but lack the knowledge of teaching or understanding of differentiated instruction.

One avenue in which to address the standards and prescribed curriculum is to encourage collaboration between teachers to learn how to differentiate instruction for their students. One teacher cannot be expected to know how to develop and implement different levels of instruction for all standards at the grade level in which she or he teaches. Working with other teachers at the same or even different grade levels can inform and allow for adaptation. In 2004, Hoover and Patton presented a way of differentiating standards based on the students' current developmental level and ability to synthesize the concepts. This differentiating of standards also involves using alternative assessments to measure the students' growth and progress on meeting the standards. Through working as a team with other teachers, the different levels of instruction can be planned and implemented. Teachers need to continually adapt the standards to meet the students' level of understanding. For this complex level of differentiation, teachers need both content knowledge as presented earlier as well as knowledge of teaching strategies. Preservice teachers should receive college preparation to meet differentiated learning needs, and in-service teachers should receive professional development to advance the learning of all students. We feel that if teachers have both content knowledge and knowledge of different teaching levels and strategies and the freedom to adapt the curriculum, the needs of all students along the continuum will be met.

Proposed Funding to Meet the Needs of Diverse Learners

The *Blueprint* (U.S. Department of Education, 2010) acknowledges the need for funding programs for diverse students. It is further noted that the funding for programs focusing on students with disabilities has historically come through the Individuals with Disabilities Education Act. President Obama has proposed that the nation increase this support to

> help ensure that teachers and leaders are better prepared to meet the needs of diverse learners, that assessments more accurately and appropriately measure the performance of students with disabilities, and that more districts and schools implement high-quality, state- and locally-determined curricula and instructional supports that incorporate the principles of universal design for learning to meet all students' needs. (p. 20)

Yet the proposed funding for IDEA state grants in 2010 remained the same as the amount in 2009 (Office of Special Education, 2011). Where is the support for special education?

Students with disabilities are included in this proposal, along with English-language learners and homeless children. However, there is very little acknowledgment of students who are high-ability learners (gifted and talented). In reality, the one very minor mention of gifted students represents no more than an afterthought. The facts are that the *funding* for the Jacob K. Javits Gifted and Talented Students Education Act, the only funding provided for high-ability students, is proposed to be cut to $0 (National Association for Gifted Children, 2010). The purpose of this subpart of the No Child Left Behind (NCLB) legislation is to provide resources to supply programming that meets the special educational needs of gifted and talented students across the nation (NGAC, 2010). Without any acknowledgment of the diverse needs of high-ability students, whether direct or indirect (through funding), teachers are forced to provide as best they can without training or resources. Although President Obama (2006) declared that "Our task, then, is to identify those reforms that have the highest impact on student achievement, fund them adequately, and eliminate those programs that don't produce results" (p. 191), when he developed his new agenda outlined in the *Blueprint* (U.S. Department of Education, 2010), the programs will not be adequately funded, and the approaches suggested, particularly for high-ability students, are vaguely outlined at best.

Success or Failure

Our opening examples of Ryan and Matt illustrate the difficulties encountered when labeling a child a success or failure, particularly based on one test score, a snapshot of his or her entire year's effort. One area of the *Blueprint* (U.S. Department of Education, 2010) that does give us cause for hope is the proposed changes to the assessment process. Recognition has been made that "most school districts rely solely on test scores to measure teacher performance, and that test scores may be highly dependent on factors beyond any teacher's control, like the number of low-income or special-needs students in their classroom" and more "meaningful, performance-based assessments" (Obama, 2006, p. 193) are needed to accurately evaluate student and teacher performance.

The administration asserts, "State accountability systems will be asked to recognize progress and growth and reward success, rather than only identify failure" (U.S. Department of Education, 2010, p. 9). We support this ideal of growth! One alternative to the one snapshot is to measure each student's individual progression through the year or semester. We suggest that students should be given routine pre- and post-assessments throughout the academic period. The proficiency score should then be based on their improvement over the semester, not how well they scored on one single test. The stories of Ryan and Matt illustrate why we must assess students on their individual growth and progress instead of measuring every student by one standard or goal. Students with disabilities may never pass the test at their grade level because of their learning differences. However, they do grow and progress. The *Blueprint* (U.S. Department of Education, 2010) supports this individual measurement: "Improved assessments can be used to accurately measure student growth; to better measure how states, districts, schools, principals, and teachers are educating students; to help teachers adjust and focus their teaching; and to provide better information to students and their families" (p. 11). We feel that with this measurement of growth, each student along the continuum of learning will be able to be called a "success" and hopefully challenged at his or her *own* developmental level.

Bridging the Gap

Collaboration provides a vital component that effective schools can use to meet the needs of all students. In the *Blueprint* (U.S. Department of Education, 2010), the administration contends that collaboration and professional development opportunities are keys to effective teachers, leaders, and schools. President Obama asserted that, "We have to do more to ensure that every student has an effective teacher, every school has effective leaders, and every teacher and leader has access to the preparation, on-going support, recognition, and collaboration opportunities he or she needs to succeed" (U.S. Department of Education, 2010, p. 13). We whole-heartedly concur with his sentiments.

When asked, teachers had many ideas of how collaboration has benefited both them and their students. In the following stories, the teachers share their perceptions of the benefits of collaboration as a whole.

> I think it is better for everybody. It makes me a better teacher because I want to bring new ideas to the group....I think it is better for my kids. They benefit not only from the experience from their one teacher, but from the experiences of the two other teachers and lots of times they benefit from another classroom trying it and it being successful or not successful and that teacher sharing. Well, I think overall, when the kids are benefiting then everybody benefits. That's the whole idea. I think when the kids benefit, then the family benefits, and then the whole community benefits. (Cindy, veteran kindergarten teacher)

I think from my standpoint moving from another grade level, this has been a "God send." Because otherwise I would have felt like I was flopping around out there like a fish out of water. And nobody had a lifeline. I really do think when we get a chance to share ideas or a little trick to share that is great….You can't be up on all of these things, it is impossible and you would make yourself crazy trying to. So this is great, we can take an idea and tweak it for ourselves. I think it benefits our kids. We all teach a little bit differently, but we all bring that to the table….So we can all benefit our kids, which is why we teach. (Amy, a veteran first-grade teacher at a new grade level)

These two teachers share how collaboration makes each of them a better teacher and is a "God send" for them to perform their duties effectively. Teachers cannot be expected to know all the content and strategies to meet the complex needs of all students. Collaboration allows them to combine their knowledge and experiences. The following stories illustrate how collaboration was beneficial for the students in the classroom.

My favorite teacher to collaborate with is a ninth-grade English teacher. Before we co-teach the class, we get together to talk about what we feel are our areas of strength and weaknesses, then we teach the parts of the class that involve more of our strength areas. An example is that I teach the vocabulary lessons and she teaches the grammar lessons. She will also teach more of the mythology and Shakespeare literature in the course, while I will teach the sections on fiction and nonfiction. I believe that all students benefit by having different strategies and teaching methods demonstrated in the classroom. The students who benefit the most are the students with disabilities and struggling students not identified as Exceptional Children. These students get more individualized help in the classroom. They get the benefit that if they do not learn the material the way one teacher teaches it, they have another teacher with ideas to help them grasp the material and succeed in the class. I have seen many successes where students succeed in a classroom with two teachers collaborating and sharing different strategies to help students with different learning styles succeed. (Rebecca, high school special education resource specialist)

The kids understand their stomachs. Even though they are in the sixth grade, some students still struggle with fractions. I was having trouble coming up with a way to reach them. Our resource teacher [the Special Education Resource Teacher] and I talked about it and came up with the idea of using McDonald's third pounders and quarter pounders. The kids couldn't figure out why a third pounder would cost more than a quarter pounder—3 is less than 4. As the resource teacher told the story, I drew visuals on the Smartboard that compared the sizes of 1/3 and 1/4 and hamburger sizes. The kids got it. (Amber, sixth-grade mathematics teacher in an elementary school)

These stories exemplify the ideal of collaboration between professionals using their strengths of content knowledge with the appropriate knowledge of multiple teaching strategies to meet the needs of all students in the inclusive classroom. Collaboration allows these teachers to use the required state standards and their strengths to co-teach students for the maximum effective production of knowledge and mastery from the students. This connects with the *Blueprint* (U.S. Department of Education, 2010) statements on progress of growth; we support that avenue of testing and applaud the concept of individual growth, not a fixed number on an arbitrary test. These situations share that the teachers were more concerned about how the students "got it" and their individual growth than about what the state standard said had to be covered. If teachers are given the opportunities and flexibility to collaborate with other professionals, just imagine the possibilities. The students would learn content, pass the tests, and still enjoy the process of learning at their individual levels of growth. Isn't that what school should be—a place to love to learn, not just a series of tests to pass?

Professional Development

Collaboration is a developed skill that requires professional instruction to be effective. As noted by the *Blueprint* (U.S. Department of Education, 2010):

> School districts may use funds to develop and implement fair and meaningful teacher and principal evaluation systems, working in collaboration with teachers, principals, and other stakeholders; to foster and provide collaboration and development opportunities in schools and build instructional teams of teachers, leaders, and other school staff, including paraprofessionals; to support educators in improving their instructional practice through effective, ongoing, job-embedded, professional development that is targeted to student and school needs; and to carry out other activities to improve the effectiveness of teachers, principals, and other school staff, and ensure the equitable distribution of effective teachers and principals. (p. 15)

There are multiple models of improvement and professional development for teachers, administrators, and schools. One school chose the learning communities' model described in *Whatever It Takes: How Professional Learning Communities Respond When Kids Don't Learn* (Dufour, Dufour, Eaker, & Karhanek, 2004). The principal in this school sees the value of support for collaboration and professional development to meet the needs of her entire staff. As she explains it, when we collaborate we have a "collective intelligence" as described in the Dufour book. She feels collaboration among her teachers leads to student improvement.

Several school districts in Indiana have utilized an early release day or late arrival day once per week to offer collaboration training and time. These routinely scheduled days and times allow for general education and special education teachers, paraprofessionals, administrators, and other school personnel (i.e., teacher-librarians) to meet and discuss how to more effectively carry out their responsibilities toward educating America's children. Teachers and administrators have expressed that these collaboration times have proved beneficial for advancing the practices and strategies of teachers to meet the needs of all students and improved student achievement. Just as medical doctors share patient information for more effective treatment of patients, teachers need to share vital information about students to best meet the many complexities of student learning. To effectively teach, you need knowledge of the whole child—knowledge of content and strategies as well as knowledge of how students interact in their environment.

Recent research points to improved student achievement when teachers and resource personnel collaborate. Achterman and Loertscher (2008) specifically looked at how teachers and teacher-librarians collaborated on implementing individual student research projects. The collaborative efforts resulted in students demonstrating a deeper understanding of the content of their research subjects, and the overall class test scores were higher for the collaborative unit of study than for previous units. The teachers were able to meet the requirements for the content presented, and student understanding was improved. Another study looked at struggling students' performance in inclusive classrooms where the general education teachers and the special education teachers collaborated to address students' goals. Hunt, Soto, Maier, and Doering's (2003) study found that in the inclusive classrooms, the teachers documented increased student engagement, self-confidence, and improvements in reading, writing, and math scores. These increased scores were reported for all struggling students. These two studies provide evidence to support the idea that collaborative teams are beneficial for teachers to become better teachers and students to gain a deeper understanding of the content and improved self-confidence.

Suggestions for Preparing Teachers

We feel that to be effective teachers for all students along the continuum of learning, teacher preparation programs need to include instruction for the differentiation of learning activities, appropriate teaching strategies, content knowledge, and skills for collaborating with other professionals. Teachers need to be exposed to the multiple ways to teach students who learn at all levels of development and have diverse learning styles and abilities. Without this knowledge and skills in how to differentiate instruction, today's teachers are often at a deficit in how to meet the needs of their diverse student population. Once again, collaboration provides one useful tool for teachers to gain these needed skills.

The *Blueprint* (U.S. Department of Education, 2010) establishes the importance of content knowledge for teachers, and we support content knowledge as a key component of teaching. However, because most teachers will have students all along the continuum of learning, they need to have knowledge of the subjects that they teach but must also understand appropriate teaching methods to assist students in a deeper understanding of the content. A symbiotic relationship is needed between the content knowledge and the methods with which to teach the content to all students. It does no good for teachers to know how to solve algebraic equations if they do not know how to teach this skill to their diverse students. Content knowledge does not guarantee an automatic transference of knowledge to the students.

Collaboration skills are vital to working with others for the common goal of meeting students' needs. At our regional university campus in Indiana, a required course for all special education teacher candidates is a course on collaboration and service delivery models. This course addresses the many complexities of working with others who are educated and devoted to their profession. We stress that you have to know your own strengths and weaknesses before you can effectively work with others. Throughout the course, we practice skills of mediation and discussion for the "win-win" scenario. Adults in the school environment need to work collaboratively to develop the skills of negotiation to be successful in meeting all needs. We believe that the collaboration course would be a value for all teacher education candidates, not just the teacher candidates in special education.

Conclusion

More than four decades ago, the first special education law, P.L. 94-142, mandated that schools must provide a continuum of educational services for students with Individualized Education Plans (IEPs), which allows students to be educated in the Least Restrictive Environment (LRE) (Ed.gov., 2010). We decree that this continuum of educational services and the LRE should be a right of all students. As a nation, why would we want to push our children into a "one-size-fits-all" educational system and restrict our students from achieving to their fullest potential? If we do not change the methods in which our children are taught and the assessments with which we measure our children, we will be forcing all of our children to learn in the *most restrictive environment*. In America, we value uniqueness and challenge our children to stand up for our values of democracy, yet we push our children to become automatons when we consider the public school systems. We must learn how to appreciate each child as a unique individual who has something beneficial to contribute to our society and respond accordingly. As educators of children, we have to be the voices that speak for our future: our children.

References

Achterman, D., & Loertscher, D. V. (2008). Where in the role are you anyway? *California School Library Association Journal, 31*(2), 10–13.

Dufour, R., Dufour, R., Eaker, R., & Karhanek, G. (2004).*Whatever it takes: How professional learning communities respond when kids don't learn.* Bloomington, IN: Solution Tree.

Ed. gov. (2010). *History: Twenty-five years of progress in educating children with disabilities through IDEA.* Available at http://www2.ed.gov/policy/speced/leg/idea/history.html

Hoover, J. J., & Patton, J. R. (2004). Differentiating standards-based education for students with diverse needs. *Remedial and Special Education, 25*(2), 74–78.

Hunt, P., Soto, G., Maier, J., & Doering, K. (2003). Collaborative teaming to support students at risk and students with severe disabilities in general education classrooms. *Exceptional Children, 69*(3), 315–332.

Indiana State Board of Education. (2000). *Indiana's academic standards.* Indianapolis, IN.

National Association for Gifted Children. (2010). Available at http://www.nagc.org/index2. aspx?id=585&al. NAGC Legislative Advocacy

Obama, B. (2006). *The audacity of hope.* New York: Random House.

Office of Special Education and Rehabilitative Services. (2011). Special education—Grants to states. Available at http://www2.ed.gov/programs/osepgts/funding.html

U.S. Department of Education. (2010, March). *A blueprint for reform: The reauthorization of elementary and secondary education act.* Washington, DC: Author.

PART III

Overview

The final two chapters in the book address instructional strategies for re-skilling our teachers and students in two content areas that have received the lion's share of attention and criticism: literacy and mathematics. Il-Hee Kim, in "Developing Critical Thinking Skills in a the Age of President Obama" (Chapter 6), takes a critical look at the imbalance in our pedagogical practic-es when we spend too much time focused on filling in bubbles on standard-ized tests and not enough time cultivating the critical thinking and reasoning skills of our students. Such deskilling is not conducive to helping our stu-dents become democratic citizens who can make a sound judgment in the 21st century. It also decreases students' motivation and engagement in read-ing and thinking. As a way to reskill our students, Kim introduces the Col-laborative Reasoning approach to discourse in the classroom, which can shift more attention toward the kinds of thinking that lead to genuine cognitive and civic development.

Keith Howard's chapter, "Hybrid Technology Classrooms for Mathemat-ics Instruction" (Chapter 7), examines our nation's preparedness to utilize its investment in technology to improve our instruction in mathematics. Despite massive federal and state investments in technology for education, we have yet to see significant changes in the achievement levels of students who are tied to that investment. In actual classrooms, the technology for math has often been used to reinforce simple calculation skills or provide drilling prac-tices, which merely deskills our students and leads them to lose interest in math. In this chapter, Howard provides an example of an effective approach that utilizes technology for reskilling our teachers and students in learning math. This approach considers the importance of basic skills in achieving proficiency in mathematics, but it also maintains commitment to allowing teachers to spend more time teaching concepts than drilling and correcting responses. This balanced approach recognizes that students need both skills and conceptual understanding to become the thinkers and problem solvers of the future. By presenting these instructional approaches for reskilling, Kim and Howard also provide hope for our classroom: With the proper use of technology and collaborative discussion, we can still help our students develop higher order thinking and reasoning skills and become intelligent and responsible citizens.

Developing Critical Thinking Skills in the Age of President Obama

Il-Hee Kim

The development of critical thinking has been an ambition of American schools since the founding of the republic. According to Thomas Jefferson, general education should "enable every man to judge for himself what will secure or endanger his freedom" (as cited in Karp, 1985, p. 70). The National Assessment of Educational Progress (NAEP) Civics Framework (National Assessment Governing Board, 2006) states:

> Intellectual and participatory civic skills involve the use of knowledge to think and act effectively and in a reasoned manner in response to the challenges of life in a constitutional democracy. Intellectual skills enable students to learn and apply civic knowledge in the many and varied roles of citizens. These skills help citizens identify, describe, explain, and analyze information and arguments, as well as evaluate, take, and defend positions on public issues. (p. x)

Today, the development of critical thinking still remains a pressing national educational goal. In an address to the U.S. Hispanic Chamber of Commerce (CNN, 2010), President Obama urged states to develop standards "that don't simply measure whether students can fill in a bubble on a test but whether they possess 21st century skills like problem-solving and critical thinking, entrepreneurship and creativity." To help promote this goal, Obama said he would push for funding in the No Child Left Behind (NCLB) law to be more effectively tied to results.

Despite the high value placed on critical thinking, nationwide assessments consistently indicate that most students cannot or do not think deeply or well and have not mastered the skills of critical thinking and reasoning skills. According to a NAEP report (Lee, Grigg, & Donahue, 2007), 33% of fourth graders are unable to grasp even the basic meaning of what they read while 75% are unable to satisfactorily make inferences, make connections to their own experiences, and draw conclusions. Very few (8%) are able to approach a text critically, explain their judgments, make generalizations, or discern deeper meanings (National Assessment Governing Board, 2007). At the eighth grade, 27% of students are able to demonstrate a strong understanding of the text and make valid inferences and meaningful connections. Only 2% can judge texts critically and extend their meaning by integrating personal experiences and other readings (Lee et al., 2007). At the high school level, the nationwide ACT exam reveals that fewer than 25% students have reading skills proficient enough to comprehend college-level text materials (ACT, 2010). Thus, national assessments indicate that across grade levels, only a small percentage of students display a high level of comprehension and critical reading skills.

One of the reasons that there are so few students showing a high level of thinking may be that the NCLB Act has led state and local curriculum to put much more emphasis on teaching basic skills than on promoting higher order thinking skills (Wenglinsky, 2004). NCLB has provided professional development funds that exclusively support a basic skills approach. The Obama administration is currently in the process of revising NCLB and emphasizes development of critical thinking skills in American education. At the same time, the administration places more accountability on teachers for students' achievement and academic performance. Some educators may suspect that instruction focusing on critical thinking skills may lower students' scores in the standardized assessments. It seems that NCLB has fostered a mistaken notion among educators that focusing on basic skills is likely to enhance students' test scores while emphasis on higher order thinking is not. However, the national assessments like NAEP (Campbell, Hombo, & Mazzeo, 2000) indicate that the instructional approaches emphasizing meaning and higher order thinking actually improve students' academic performance. For instance, with regard to mathematics, instructions centered on project-based learning, higher order thinking skills, and problems that have more than one solution are all associated with higher performance on the mathematics NAEP. With regard to science, fourth-grade students tended to perform better on the NAEP science tests when they had engaged in projects in which they took a high degree of initiative. Simply filling out the worksheets and identifying information from the textbooks did not seem to have much positive effect on students' learning. The NAEP reading tests also revealed similar results: Students tended to score higher on comprehension questions when they had experienced instruction that involves practice on metacognitive comprehension skills, such as thinking critically about the author's intention. These NAEP scores suggest that in order to enhance comprehension of the texts, students should develop critical thinking skills.

Therefore, to improve students' academic performance and civic education, critical thinking skills should be emphasized in a school curriculum and should be addressed in a proposed education reform by the Obama administration. Like other skills, critical thinking skills should be fostered from early childhood and actively practiced in elementary school students. Students should be taught from a young age how to think critically about the matters at hand and how to make a sound judgment using available information and resources.

This chapter deals with the development of critical thinking skills among elementary school students. It first describes what theorists have suggested with regard to developing children's critical thinking skills. Then it examines a prevalent classroom practice and presents the Collaborative Reasoning approach as an alternative way to stimulate thinking skills. Then it provides practical guidelines to teachers, educators, and administrators about how to implement the Collaborative Reasoning approach.

Theories of Development of Children's Thinking Skills

Theories of developing children's thinking skills can be traced back to Piaget (1965), who notes that when children cooperate with their peers, their reasoning and critical thinking skills are likely to develop. From a developmental perspective, Piaget suggests that the development of children's thinking requires a transition from an egocentric stage to a cooperation stage, and collaborating with peers helps children objectify themselves. During peer interaction, children may bring different perspectives to a problem, which creates cognitive conflicts with their own thinking. While trying to resolve those conflicts with their peers, children compare their thoughts with others and come to view themselves from a more objective point of view. Because there is no answer easily agreed on about those conflicts, the children tend to argue their position and convince others with sound evidence and reasons. Those conflicts also increase the likelihood of negotiation and active interaction. Rogoff (1990) also indicates that peer interaction, especially group discussions, enhances children's reasoning skills. Based on previous empirical studies, Rogoff suggests that children who have participated in collaborative problem solving tend to show a greater improvement in their level of thinking than those who have never collaborated at all. She also points out that children who discuss their ideas with each other are likely to improve their individual level of logic.

Like Piaget (1965), Vygotsky (1978) argues that individual reasoning processes first emerge in social interaction with others. According to Vygotsky, the reasoning skills gained through social interaction are internalized by the individual. Wertch (1985) rephrases this idea by saying, "All higher mental functions appear first on the interpsychological plane and then on the intrapsychological plane" (p. 158). Thus, to promote children's intrapsychological thinking, the social context that involves interpsychological activities, such as group discussions, should be provided first. Vygotsky argues that children's speech in the egocentric stage that Piaget hypothesizes should be regarded as a transitional form from external to internal speech. When the external or socialized speech turns inward, that is, when language comes to play an intrapersonal function from interpersonal one, children begin to use language as a thinking tool and develop their reasoning skills. Vygotsky even regards thinking as a dialogue with oneself and thoughts as outputs from internalized dialogues. In a similar vein, Bakhtin (1981) proposes that reasoning is inherently dialogical, and Anderson et al. (2001) argues that to develop thinking skills, "thinkers must hear several voices within their own heads representing different perspectives on the issue" (p. 2). A group discussion can provide such a context in which children engage in a series of dialogues with their peers who hold different perspectives.

Whereas Vygotsky (1978) emphasizes the role of language in a transition from interpsychological function to intrapsychological function, Wertch (1985) stresses the importance of intersubjectivity. Wertch points out that when children enter into a communicative context, they may have different interpretations about the situation, event, or objects, but "through semiotically mediated 'negotiation,' they create a temporarily shared social world, a state of intersubjectivity" (p. 161). That is, children who collaborate in a social context initially bring divergent interpretations about the situation and face the problem of establishing intersubjectivity. Through reciprocal communication and meaningful negotiation, they go beyond their "private" perspective and come to share the interpretation of the situation. Rogoff (1990) supports the importance of intersubjectivity by addressing its cognitive benefits. She finds that the intersubjectivity between mothers and young children during conversations in a museum led to greater memory for the information discussed. She suggests that interaction in which the adult and the child manage to achieve intersubjectivity may enhance the child's subsequent performance. In relation to intersubjectivity, Rogoff also suggests the importance of joint problem solving. She evidences that the children who worked on problem-solving tasks with peers and shared decision making performed better than those who worked alone or did not share their decisions. She further demonstrates that children who discussed their opinions and shared decision making on a logic game improved more than those who did not. She concludes that "the most productive interaction appears to result from arrangements in which peers' decision making occurs jointly" (p. 163).

In summary, these theories all suggest that sharing ideas through interaction is essential for children's development of thinking skills. In other words, engaging students in a group discussion is an effective way to foster critical thinking skills. However, as Rogoff (1990) suggests, the group discussion may not improve children's thinking ability unless the children share their decisions and actually work jointly to solve the problem or issue. Although children actively participate in group discussions, they will not gain much from the peer interaction if they insist only that their own ideas are valid without paying attention to others' or if they fail to achieve a shared understanding about the problem through meaningful negotiation. The quality of a discussion is also important for higher order of thinking. Students' talks during the discussion should involve deeper thought processes and critical evaluations of the information.

Then, what are the current practices of discussions in schools? Are these practices congruent with what the theorists have suggested? In the next section, we examine a prevalent form of group discussion in an elementary classroom and explore an effective way to foster critical thinking skills among children.

Current Practices of Classroom Discussions

Unfortunately, the research shows that such dialogic learning using discussion methods is not prevalent in the schools. Nystrand, Wu, Gamoran, Zeiser, and Long (2003) found that only about 6.7% of instructional conversations contained even one "dialogic spell" or interval of discussion in which there was an in-depth exchange of ideas. The dialogic spells that did occur occupied only a few fleeting moments. Furthermore, the research shows that most elementary classroom discussions provide little or no opportunity for extended thinking. The following discussion transcript, illustrated in Clark et al. (2003), shows a typical discussion pattern found in elementary classrooms. For the discussion, the students read the story *Ronald Morgan Goes to Bat* (Giff, 1990), which is about a boy who likes to play baseball. He is a poor player, but he encourages other team members all the time.

T: Who is the main character of this story?

S: Ronald.

T: Yes, and what was the problem he faced in this story?

S: He couldn't do anything right.

T: No, what was he trying to do?

S: He was trying to play baseball.

T: Yes, so, our stories usually have a problem and a solution. Remember? We talked about that yesterday. So what was the problem in this story?

S: (no response)

T: Ok, B. Can you help S. out?

B: He wanted to play, but he ran the bases backward and closed his eyes so he couldn't hit the ball.

T: Ok, J, what else did he do wrong?

J: He drew letters in the mud with a stick?

T: Why is that a problem?

B: He wasn't paying attention to what his coach was telling him?

T: Ok, so the problem in the story was that he couldn't do the things he was supposed to be able to do to play ball, he couldn't hit, he couldn't run, and he didn't pay attention. Is that a problem when you want to play ball?

Class: (in unison) Yeeeeesss.

T: So the problem Ronald faced in this story was he kept making mistakes every time he tried to play ball. What happened next?

Note. T = Teacher; B, S, J, G, K... = Students. (Clark et al., 2003, p. 182)

This type of discussion approach is called recitation, in which a teacher usually initiates the discussion and asks students questions about the story they have read (Anderson, Chinn, Waggoner, & Nguyen, 1998). As shown in the transcript, in recitations, the teacher controls turn taking and talks most during the discussion (Cazden, 2001). Only a few students in a group respond to the teacher's questions, and there are few peer-to-peer interactions during the recitations. The teacher seems to have an interpretive authority on the text and evaluates students' answers. According to Cazden (2001), this "three-part sequence of teacher Initiation, student Response, and teacher Evaluation (IRE) or teacher Feedback (IRF), may still be the most common classroom discourse pattern at all grade levels. It is certainly the oldest, with a long and hardy life through many decades of formal Western-type schooling" (p. 30). Because it is so widespread and long lived, she refers to the IRE or IRF as the "default option" or the "traditional lesson structure" (Cazden, 2001, p. 131). Most classroom discussions are really recitations in the IRE format during which the teacher typically quizzes students about facts in reading material. This kind of discussion does not set the stage for thoughtful, elaborated student talk. Previous research has shown that the recitation does not lead to much cognitive development (Onosko, 1990) and does not promote the higher level of student–teacher interaction (Nystrand et al., 2003). The following section introduces an alternative approach to the recitation in elementary student education.

Collaborative Reasoning Approach for Developing Critical Thinking Skills

In the following discussion, the students read the same story *Ronald Morgan Goes to Bat* (Giff, 1990), but they are given the big question for the discussion: Should the coach let Ronald play on the team?

T: The big question is, Should the coach let Ronald play?

S: I don't think so because he couldn't do anything right.

L: Yeah, if he was on a team, he would make people lose.

R: Nobody would want to pick him.

J: I think he should have a chance to be on the team because then he might have a chance to get better.

B: That wouldn't be fair because he would make everybody lose in the meantime.

A: Winning isn't everything.

T: So. What do you think? Should the coach let Ronald play?

A: Maybe the coach could get his dad to practice with him.

G: When I first started playing baseball, I was scared I'd get hit by the ball so I wasn't very good at first, but then after a few practices I got better. I wasn't as…

K: How would you feel if nobody wanted you to play and called you "four eyes" just because you wore glasses? I think they ought to let him play.

B: But the rest of the team would have to suffer until he got better. Wouldn't that make him feel pretty bad? It would me!

A: I think he deserves a chance.

B: I disagree because no one would like him then.

Note. T = Teacher; B, S, J, G, K... = Students. (Clark et al., 2003, p. 182)

This discussion method is called Collaborative Reasoning (CR), which is intended to stimulate critical reading and thinking and to be personally engaging (Chinn, Anderson, & Waggoner, 2001; Clark et al., 2003; Kim, Anderson, Nguyen-Jahiel, & Archodidou, 2007; Nguyen-Jahiel, Anderson, Waggoner, & Rowell, 2007; Waggoner, Chinn, Yi, & Anderson, 1995). This approach has been developed by Richard Anderson and his research team (e.g., Anderson, Chinn, Chang, Waggoner, & Yi, 1997). In the CR approach, students gather in small, heterogeneous groups for a discussion in which they are expected to take positions on a "big question" raised by the story, present reasons and evidence for their positions, and challenge one another when they disagree. CR is not about reaching a consensus nor is it a debate in which one side wins and the other loses. Students are supposed to cooperatively search for good solutions to the characters' dilemma. They weigh reasons and evidence and individually decide whether to maintain or change their positions on the big question.

As seen from the transcript, in the CR discussion, there are only 2 teacher turns and 12 student turns. This contrasts with the recitation discussion shown earlier, in which there are 9 teacher turns and 7 student turns. In recitation, only 3 students contribute to the discussion, but in the CR discussion, 8 students contribute to the discussion. Thus, in a CR discussion, the majority of students in a group tend to be actively involved in sharing their ideas and thoughts about the issues, whereas the recitation elicits responses from only a few students in a group, and thus it is not likely to promote a higher level of thinking skills among students (Rogoff, 1990).

Empirical studies have been conducted to compare the effects of the CR method with those of the conventional approach to story discussion in classroom practice. Anderson et al. (1998) found that in comparison with the recitations, CR discussions produced more complex patterns of interaction between the teacher and the students and greater engagement among students. As compared with recitation, during collaborative reasoning discussion, students tended to ask more questions to the teacher, express their positions, suggest new ideas, and challenge or support the teacher's arguments. Anderson et al. also noticed more interjections and back-channeling comments such as "Uh-huh" and "Right" between students and the teacher. They also found that during CR discussions, as the amount of teacher's talk was reduced, the amount of students' talk significantly increased, and more student–student turn sequences rather than teacher–student ones were detected during the discussions.

In addition to the increased quantity of students' participation, the quality of students' social interaction was also higher during CR discussions. Chinn et al. (2001) observed that during CR discussions, students were involved in a more advanced level of cognitive interaction than during the traditional recitation discussions. Students not only built on each other's knowledge to co-construct ideas but also critiqued each other's ideas. Similarly, Chinn and Anderson (1998) found that CR discussions led students to actively collaborate on the construction of the argument in complex networks of reasons and supporting evidence. Waggoner et al. (1995) noted that the level of students' reasoning was high during CR discussions. The children who participated in CR discussions tended to elaborate ideas by linking them to prior knowledge, draw inferences that connect different parts of texts they read, recognize the importance of clarity, and advance ingenious ideas in support of their positions. According to Hofer and Pintrich (1997), those mental processes indicated that children acquired the metacognitive ability to reflect on their own thinking. Brown and Palincsar (1989) claimed that the ability to monitor one's own mental activities is essential for successful learning and higher order thinking.

One of the noteworthy findings with regard to a CR discussion is that students who participated in oral CR discussions wrote better argumentative essays than students who did not (e.g., Reznitskaya et al., 2001). The essays written by CR students contained a significantly greater number of arguments, counterarguments, rebuttals, uses of formal argument devices, and references to text information than those written by control group students who did not experience CR. This finding has been replicated in several studies (e.g., Kuo, Kim, Wu, & Dong, 2006). The following essay illustrates the typical level of written argumentation that students were able to achieve after experiencing the CR discussions. The spelling has been corrected, but the content and grammar have been left unchanged. The writing prompt was a story, not used for CR discussions, about Jack and Thomas who are competing in a soap box derby. Thomas wins the race, but he breaks the rules by not making his car by himself, and he confides this secret to Jack. The question students consider is whether Jack should tell on Thomas.

> I think Jack should not tell on Thomas. It said in the story that he had never won anything. It looked like Thomas was getting some friends and if Jack tattled Thomas would lose them. There would be other chances for Jack to win something. Some people might say that Thomas doesn't deserve the prize. But Thomas was poor because it said he smelled strange. Thomas was mean because he didn't have any friends. I think Jack should let Thomas win the prize. But someone might say that Thomas has been mean and Jack should tell. The reason Thomas is mean is because no one is nice to him. But some people might say that it meant a lot to Jack and that Thomas did not put much effort. (Which is true). This might change my mind.

In this essay, the student clearly states his position, provides supporting arguments, and considers and rebuts counterarguments. In addition to citing textual evidence, the student appeals to hypothetical situations and general principles. He seems to anticipate opposing arguments, as shown in the repeated phrases, "Some people might say." He seems to be engaged in a dialog with "some people" throughout the writing process. The student also appears to be open to alternative perspectives, which are being integrated with the chosen position. Importantly, the student's position on the issue is tentative as indicated by the last sentence. He is willing to reevaluate his position when he finds a compelling argument on the other side. This essay reflects the development of critical thinking skills through participation in a series of CR discussions. Because no formal lesson for argumentative essay writing was given to the participating children in the studies, the high frequency of argumentative elements in CR students' essays may be primarily attributed to the carryover effects of engaging in CR discussions. This is consistent with Vygotsky's (1978) general law of cultural development, which suggests that all higher mental function appears on the interpsychological plane first and then transforms to the intrapsychological plane. The interpsychological plane is where social interaction occurs, and a CR discussion provides such a social context for a child. The reasoning and thinking skills that a child has acquired during the CR discussion are likely to transfer to the intrapsychological plane, a child's internal mental organization.

In a meta-analysis, Murphy, Wilkinson, Soter, Hennessey, and Alexander (2009) compared nine popular discussion approaches for elementary students. The results of the analysis show that many of the approaches were highly effective at promoting students' literal and inferential comprehension, but relatively few of the approaches were particularly effective at promoting students' critical thinking, reasoning, and argumentation about and around text. Murphy et al. (2009) also found that in most discussion approaches, student talk increased while teacher talk decreased, but increases in student talk did not necessarily lead to improvement in student comprehension. They found that among these nine approaches, the CR approach is the most effective in promoting critical thinking, reasoning, and argumentation about and around text that students have read.

These results all support the usefulness of CR approaches in developing critical thinking skills. The next section presents the elements, features, and procedures of the CR discussion approach.

Framework of Collaborative Reasoning Discussion

Procedures of Discussion

CR discussions follow seven basic steps (Clark et al., 2003):

1. Students read the text for discussion.
2. Students gather in small groups for discussion.
3. After reviewing the discussion rules (as listed below), the teacher poses a Big Question related to the story they have read. Students announce their initial positions to the Big Question.
4. Students freely present reasons and evidence to support their initial positions.
5. Students evaluate and challenge the arguments and respond to counterarguments. Students may change their minds during the discussion.
6. Students present their final position.
7. The teacher debriefs with students about the discussion. They discuss how to improve future discussions.

The following are the detailed guidelines for each step.

Reading the text for discussion. Students should read the text before they gather in their groups so they have plenty of time to think about the issues raised in the text. Students read silently by themselves or in pairs. Although some teachers like to use round-robin reading, research has found that student attention wanders during round-robin reading, and nonfluent readers tend to get embarrassed during oral reading (Cohen & Cowen, 2011).

Gathering in small groups for discussion. When possible, students should be organized in heterogeneous groups, balanced by gender and mixed on their reading levels, as well as social dispositions, such as shy or outgoing. The heterogeneity brings diverse ideas and perspectives to the group discussion. The previous studies found that low-achieving students often contributed much to the discussion (Clark et al., 2003). They could also learn by observing other high-achieving students' performance during the discussion. The recommended group size is between six to eight students. This size range would provide a group with enough diversity in perspectives but also enough opportunity for everyone to participate.

Initiation of discussion with the teacher's Big Question. The discussion begins with the teacher posing the Big Question. The Big Question is a central question about a significant issue raised in the text that students have read. The Big Question should be a springboard for the students to explore other related issues. Typically, the Big Question addresses a dilemma faced by the main characters in the story.

Presenting initial positions to the Big Question. After the question is posed by the teacher, students announce their initial position. Students may present a definite "yes" or "no" position, but it is also acceptable for them to present a novel position of their own or to state that they are unsure. At this point in the discussion, it is important that each student present only his or her initial position briefly without any reasons or evidence. Students can quickly find where each member of the group stands on the Big Question. The students should not rely on the thinking of others, nor should they be forced to follow other students' position. When announcing their position, students can take turns individually stating his or her position or use hand signals to indicate their positions. For example, a two-thumbs up indicates the "yes" position and a two-thumbs down signals the "no" position. If students prefer, they can use table tents to show the positions that they hold.

Providing reasons and evidence to support the initial positions. Once each student has presented his or her initial position, the teacher asks the students to provide reasons and evidence to support their position. The students may give reasons using evidence from the story, from personal experience, or from previously read texts. The teacher is supposed to provide scaffolding for good thinking and rhetorical strategies by prompting students for reasons, evidence, and challenges to others. The teacher's modeling of thinking and talking processes would be helpful for students.

Challenging the arguments and responding to the counterarguments. During the discussion, students are expected to pay attention to other students' responses and evaluate them in a critical manner. Once other students challenge their claims, they are expected to respond to those counterarguments with sound reasons and evidence. Throughout the discussion, as students listen to the arguments and challenges posed by others, they may reconsider their initial position in light of the alternative viewpoints and decide whether to maintain or change their initial positions. The purpose of the discussion is neither about reaching a consensus nor determining which side wins and which side loses. Students are supposed to collaborate with one another in order to find better solutions to the dilemma that the main character faces (Dong, Anderson, Kim, & Li, 2008). Instead of quickly reaching a consensus on the issue, the students are encouraged to explore multiple perspectives and make a careful judgment on them. The ultimate goal of the CR discussion includes "inculcating the values and habits of mind to use reasoned discourse as means for choosing among competing ideas" (Anderson et al., 1998, p. 172).

Presenting the final positions. At the end of the deliberation, the teacher asks students to summarize their discussion and has them indicate their final positions in regard to the Big Question. The students must provide a reason, presented during the discussion, that supports their position.

Debriefing. The teacher debriefs with students about the discussion. Students should review and evaluate their group performance on social interaction and argumentation. They are expected to reflect on the weaknesses and strengths of their collaboration and set goals to improve future discussions. The role of the teacher is to provide feedback on the students' reflections and help them set their goals.

Open Mode of Participation

One of the features of the CR discussion approach is open participation, in which a teacher does not control turn taking and students can speak freely without being nominated by the teacher. Students are supposed to avoid interrupting each other. Quiet students are encouraged to enter the discussion. Talkative students are encouraged to not monopolize the conversation. While students attempt to maintain the flow of the discussion, the teacher tries to reduce his or her own talk and participate in the discussion as a facilitator rather than an authoritative figure. This open participation structure was suggested by Au and Mason (1981), who conducted a pioneering study comparing the effects of teachers' different instructional patterns on native Hawaiian children. Au and Mason found that under open participation as opposed to teacher-controlled participation, Hawaiian children performed better on several measures of quantity and quality of discussion contribution. Based on the finding, they argued that higher levels of productive student behaviors are more probable under the open participation structure, in which "there is a balance between the interactional rights of the teacher and children" (p. 150). As Waggoner et al. (1995) noted, the balance of rights between the teacher and students actually increased students' access to discussions. Students who usually did not voice their ideas became more willing to participate when they had the equal right to talk. In the Kim et al. (2002) study, students said that they preferred open participation structure to teacher-controlled participation because of the balance of rights, that is, they could get the floor right away without getting permission from the teacher. Students who had experienced open participation said that the teacher's role in creating a good discussion was to act as a facilitator, whereas those who had not experienced open participation said the teacher's job was to quiz students to make sure they understand the story. Kim et al. also found that students with low reading comprehension scores were strongly influenced by experience with open participation. With no experience, students who had low reading comprehension scores preferred teacher-controlled participation, but with a few weeks of CR experience, they switched their preference to open participation. In contrast, students with high reading comprehension scores preferred open participation regardless of whether they had experienced it.

Ground Rules and Norms

To ensure that students have respectful and productive discussions, it is recommended that a teacher establish a set of ground rules and norms that everyone can agree to abide by. For example, rules of participation may state that everyone is encouraged to participate in the discussion and no one should talk while others are talking. A teacher can work with the children to modify these rules or add other rules if necessary. The teacher may also establish norms for argumentation. For instance, the teacher may emphasize that everyone should support his or her positions with reasons and evidence and consider different sides of an issue.

Before beginning the first discussion, the teacher and students should go over these rules and norms. As students become more accustomed to these rules and norms, the teacher may find it no longer necessary to remind students of the rules at the subsequent discussions. Instead of reviewing all the rules and norms at each discussion session, the teacher may ask students to identify two or three that the group has the most difficult time following and help the students set goals to adhere to them. If the teacher explains to the students the purpose of the CR discussion, especially in the first few discussions, he or she can help the students understand why they are supposed to follow such rules and make them more willing to follow the rules and norms. For example, the teacher may explain to the students, "The purpose of this discussion is not to come up with 'right' or 'wrong' answers, but to come up with the best (or better) solution, decision, or ways of thinking. You will be thinking critically about the questions, giving reasons, considering evidence for the reasons, and deciding which of the reasons are the strongest."

Teacher's Instructional Moves

While students are engaged in the CR discussion following the rules and norms, the teacher is expected to relinquish a great degree of turn-taking management and topic control over to the students. One of the major goals of the CR approach is to foster students' independence; students can carry on a discussion with little or no assistance from the teacher. Thus, in CR, the teacher plays a role of facilitator, gradually delegating the responsibility of managing a discussion to the students. From the beginning, the teacher should make it clear to the students that the CR discussion is to be their discussion, where they share their opinions on the Big Question with one another. The students are ultimately responsible for maintaining an orderly discussion, managing their own turn taking rather than relying on the teacher. Sometimes a teacher may deliberately say nothing during the discussion in order to allow children time to work through a problem themselves, although this creates a long pause in the discussion.

In addition to surrendering control over turn taking, in CR, the teacher is expected to relinquish interpretative authority, which declares that some information is accurate but other information is inaccurate (Chinn et al., 2001). The rationale is that discussion cannot be genuine when a teacher, as an authority figure, presumes to settle issues (Almasi, O'Flahavan, & Arya, 2001). In CR, the teacher is expected to allow students to have the interpretive authority to evaluate the ideas and thoughts put forth.

Although students are expected to assume the teacher's roles eventually in CR, especially at the first few discussions, the teacher should play various instructional roles to assist the development of students' critical thinking and reasoning. According to Nguyen-Jahiel et al. (2007), the teacher's major instructional roles include: (a) prompting students for their ideas and thoughts, (b) modeling reasoning processes by thinking aloud, (c) asking for clarification, (d) challenging students with counterarguments, (e) encouraging good reasoning, (f) summing up what students have said, and (g) debriefing with students. For example, if a shy student does not say anything, then the teacher may prompt by asking, "What do you think about the issue?" The teacher may demonstrate how he or she thinks about the issue in the story, using phrases such as give reasons, provide evidence, and form an argument. When students fail to consider an alternative viewpoint, the teacher may interject by stating, "But, what if…" as a way of introducing a counterargument to stimulate further discussion. In CR, a teacher may have to intervene occasionally if a discussion goes too far astray from the topic or if a student gets confused about someone's line of reasoning. The teacher may repeat the Big Question, summarize the points the students have made so far, or ask a student to clarify a position.

Specific instructional moves that the teacher makes are dependent on the progress of the discussion, the dynamics of the group, and the logical flow of argumentation. From the case study with a teacher and her fourth-grade students, Nguyen-Jahiel et al. (2007) observed that those specific instructional moves helped the veteran teacher refrain from using her conventional teacher-controlled approach and adopted a new CR approach, which encourages students' participation. While using those instructional moves, the teacher noticed a change in literature discussions in terms of the focus of the discussion and the patterns of interactions in the group. The nature of story discussions changed from teacher–student interactions to student–student exchanges and from individual student performances to multiple student collaborations.

Selection of Stories and Big Question

The stories for CR discussions are carefully chosen to contain topics that are relevant to the students and can provoke a genuine and thoughtful dialog (Reznitskaya & Anderson, 2002). The issues in the stories are widely diverse, including friendship, lying, sports, ecology, ethnic identity, animal rights, and racism. The stories for CR discussions typically feature a character facing an important decision. Usually the pressure for the character to make the decision builds to a climax, but sometimes the students are stopped from reading the end of the story, preventing them from finding out what the character decides to do. The students must then use the same information the character has access to in the story, along with understandings gleaned from their life experience, to discuss what the character should do. For example, in the story *Stone Fox* (Gardiner, 1980), Willie enters a dog race to win enough money to pay the taxes on his grandfather's farm. Stone Fox, who wins every dog race he enters, wants the prize money to continue buying land back for his native people. Willie is leading the race, but when he reaches 10 feet from the finish line, his beloved dog dies of exhaustion. For CR discussions, the students are supposed to stop reading at that moment. They are not allowed to read further or find what actually happens in the story. The Big Question is based on the dilemma faced by Stone Fox: "Should Stone Fox let Willie win the race?" A CR discussion based on *Stone Fox* can stimulate emotions, justifications, and predictions as children consider various issues related to the story. For instance, a student may argue that Stone Fox should not let Willie win the race because Native Indians should have their land returned or at least an opportunity to purchase it. Other students may disagree with the idea by saying that Willie leads the race for the most time, and Stone Fox might have a second chance in the future races, so Stone Fox should let Willie win the race. Because the Big Question involves a dilemma that has at least two plausible options, this story usually provokes a lively discussion. Children become entangled in the "trade-offs" while trying to figure out what might be the best solution to the dilemma (Clark et al., 2003). The Big Question is also formulated to elicit multiple perspectives and diverse ideas. While responding to the Big Question, students tend to present various ideas, provide supporting reasons for their ideas, and challenge one another's ideas (Chinn & Anderson, 1998). According to Anderson and Pichert (1978), sharing multiple perspectives helps students recall more items in the story that they read.

Conclusion

Theories and empirical studies of cognitive development support the idea that engaging students in a group discussion is an effective way to stimulate their thinking. Although the conventional recitation method adopts a discussion format, it mostly focuses on basic reading skills and recall of texts, but it does not contribute much to the development of children's critical thinking. In contrast, the CR approach enables children to expand their repertoire of responses to literature by learning to think in a reasoned manner and to explore diverse views prompted by what they read. The CR method also gives children greater control over interpretation, turn taking, and the topic at hand (Chinn et al., 2001). Thus, the CR approach provides children with a context in which they can be actively involved in cognitive and intellectual processes through argumentation.

Professional development programs on the CR approach should be offered to elementary school teachers so they can actually implement the approach in their instruction. The teachers should always be reminded that the ultimate purpose of education is not simply to help students achieve a high score in the standardized assessments but to help students grow up to be democratic citizens who can make sound choices regarding political, social, and personal matters. The CR approach will help students possess those skills that Obama administration regards as necessary in the 21st century.

References

ACT, Inc. (2010). *Solutions for success in an evolving global market: ACT Annual Report.* Iowa City, IA: Author.

Almasi, J. F., O'Flahavan, J. F., & Arya, P. (2001). A comparative analysis of student and teacher development in more and less proficient discussions of literature. *Reading Research Quarterly,* 36(2), 96–120.

Anderson, R. C., & Pichert, J. W. (1978). Recall of previously unrecallable information following a shift in perspective. *Journal of Verbal Learning and Verbal Behavior,* 17, 1–12.

Anderson, R. C., Chinn, C., Chang, J., Waggoner, M., & Yi, H. (1997). On the logical integrity of children's arguments. *Cognition and Instruction,* 15, 135–167.

Anderson, R. C., Chinn, C., Waggoner, M., & Nguyen, K. T. (1998). Intellectually stimulating story discussions. In J. Osborn & F. Lehr (Eds.), *Literacy for all* (pp. 170–196). New York: Guilford.

Anderson, R. C., Nguyen-Jahiel, K., McNurlen, B., Archodidou, A., Kim, S., Reznitskaya, A., et al. (2001). The snowball phenomenon: Spread of ways of talking and ways of thinking across groups of children. *Cognition and Instruction,* 19(1), 1–46.

Au, K. H., & Mason, J. M. (1981). Social organization factors in learning: The balance of rights hypothesis. *Reading Research Quarterly,* 17(1), 115–152.

Bakhtin, M. M. (1981). *The dialogic imagination: Four essays by M. M. Bakhtin.* Austin: University of Texas Press.

Brown, A. L., & Palincsar, A. S. (1989). Guided, cooperative learning and individual knowledge acquisition. In L. B. Resnick (Ed.), *Knowing, learning, and instruction: Essays in honor of Robert* Glaser (pp. 393–451). Hillsdale, NJ: Lawrence Erlbaum Associates.

Campbell, J. R., Hombo, C. M., & Mazzeo, J. (2000). *NAEP 1999 Trends in Academic Progress: Three Decades of Student Performance* (NCES 2000–469). Washington, DC: U.S. Department of Education, Office of Educational Research and Improvement, National Center for Education Statistics.

Cazden, C. (2001). *Classroom discourse: The language of teaching and learning.* Portsmouth, NH: Heinemann.

Chinn, C., & Anderson, R. C. (1998). The structure of discussions that promote reasoning. *Teachers College Record,* 100(2), 315–368.

Chinn, C. A., Anderson, R. C., & Waggoner, M. (2001). Patterns of discourse during two kinds of literature discussion. *Reading Research Quarterly,* 36, 378–411.

Clark, A.-M., Anderson, R. C., Kuo, L.-J., Kim, I.-H., Archodidou, A., & Nguyen-Jahiel, K. (2003). Collaborative reasoning: Expanding ways for children to talk and think in school. *Educational Psychology Review,* 15, 181–198.

CNN. (2010). CNN news. Available at http://www.cnn.com/2009/POLITICS/03/10/obama

.education

Cohen, V. L., & Cowen, J. E. (2011). *Literacy for children in an Information Age: Teaching reading, writing, and thinking* (2nd ed.). Belmont, CA: Wadsworth.

Dong, T., Anderson, R. C., Kim, I.-H., & Li, Y. (2008). Collaborative reasoning in China and Korea. *Reading Research Quarterly, 43*(4), 400–424.

Gardiner, J. (1980). *Stone Fox*. New York: Crowell Junior Books.

Giff, P. R. (1990). *Ronald Morgan goes to bat*. New York: Puffin.

Hofer, B. K., & Pintrich, P. R. (1997). The development of epistemological theories: Beliefs about knowledge and knowing and their relation to learning. Review of Educational Research, 67, 88–140.

Karp, W. (1985). Why Johnny can't think: The politics of bad schooling. *Harper's Magazine*, 270(1621), 69–73.

Kim, I.-H., Anderson, R. C., Nguyen-Jahiel, K., & Archodidou, A. (2007). Discourse patterns during children's collaborative online discussions. *Journal of the Learning Sciences, 16*(3), 333–370.

Kim, S., Anderson, R., McNurlen, B., Archodidou, A., Nguyen-Jahiel, K., & Reznitskaya, A. (2002). *Do fourth graders prefer open or teacher-controlled discussions?* Champaign, IL: Center for the Study of Reading.

Kuo, L.-J., Kim, I., Wu, X., & Dong, T. (2006, April). Influence of collaborative discussions on children's reflective essays. Symposium session presented at the annual meeting of American Educational Research Association, San Francisco, CA.

Lee, J., Grigg, W. S., & Donahue, P. L. (2007). *Nation's report card: Reading* (NCES 2007-496). Washington, DC: U.S. Department of Education, Institute of Education Sciences, National Center for Education Statistics.

Murphy, P. K., Wilkinson, I. A. G., Soter, A. O., Hennessey, M. N., & Alexander, J. F. (2009). Examining the effects of classroom discussion on students' high-level comprehension of text: A meta-analysis. *Journal of Educational Psychology*, 101, 740–764.

National Assessment Governing Board. (2006). *Civics framework for the 2006 National Assessment of Educational Progress*. Washington, DC: U.S. Department of Education.

National Assessment Governing Board. (2007). *Reading framework for the 2007 National Assessment of Educational Progress*. Washington, DC: U.S. Department of Education.

Nguyen-Jahiel, K., Anderson, R., Waggoner, M., & Rowell, B. (2007). Using literature discussions to reason through real life dilemmas: A journey taken by one teacher and her fourth-grade children. In R. Horowitz (Ed.), *Talking texts: How speech and writing interact in school learning*. Hillsdale, NJ: Lawrence Erlbaum Associates.

Nystrand, M., Wu, A., Gamoran, A., Zeiser, S., & Long, D. A. (2003). Questions in time: Investigating the structure and dynamics of unfolding classroom discourse. *Discourse Processes, 35*(3), 135–198.

Onosko, J. J. (1990). Comparing teachers' instruction to promote students' thinking. *Journal of Curriculum Studies*, 22, 443–461.

Piaget, J. (1965). *The moral judgment of the child* (M. Gabain, Trans.). New York: The Free Press.

Reznitskaya, A., & Anderson, R. C. (2002). The argument schema and learning to reason. In C. C. Block & M. Pressley (Eds.), *Comprehension instruction* (pp. 319–334). New York: Guilford.

Reznitskaya, A., Anderson, R. C., McNurlen, B., Nguyen-Jahiel, K., Archodidou, A., & Kim, S. (2001). Influence of oral discussion on written argument. *Discourse Processes*, 32, 155–175.

Rogoff, B. (1990). *Apprenticeship in thinking.* Oxford: Oxford University Press.

Vygotsky, L. S. (1978). *Mind in society.* Cambridge, MA: Harvard University Press.

Waggoner, M., Chinn, C., Yi, H., & Anderson, R. C. (1995). Collaborative reasoning about stories. *Language Arts*, 72, 582–589.

Wenglinsky, H. (2004). Facts or critical thinking skills? What NAEP results say. *Educational Leadership,* 62(1), 32–35.

Wertch, J. (1985). *Vygotsky and the social formation of mind.* Cambridge, MA: Harvard University Press.

CHAPTER SEVEN

Hybrid Technology Classrooms for Mathematics Instruction

Keith Howard

As we peer into today's K-12 classrooms, we witness an environment very different from what would have been observed not many years ago. Today we are more likely to see evidence of the technological advancements that have piqued the interests of people in all walks of business and personal life. It is an interest that was clearly evident when then-candidate Barack Obama spoke at a high school in Dayton, Ohio, on September 9, 2008. In a speech titled "A New Vision for a 21st Century Education," Obama called on Americans to imagine a future where our children are learning on "whiteboards with digital touch screens; where every student in a classroom has a laptop at their desk; where they don't just do book reports but design PowerPoint presentations; where they don't just write papers but build websites" (Barack in Dayton, 2008). This vision has surely manifested itself in the subsequent policy and budgetary decision making of the Obama administration. which is evident by their investment of more than half a billion dollars in educational innovation in schools and cyberlearning noted in the 2011 budget (Fletcher, 2010).

It seems that the move to put computers and many other technology-based teaching and learning tools into every classroom has marched forward with the implied belief that increased learning will surely follow. This chapter examines the effect that research suggests this movement has had and/or can have on learning. Our examination is centered on mathematics content, exploring ways that the benefits in efficiency and productivity observed in the business sector might be applied in classrooms to facilitate better, faster, and more efficient acquisition of necessary knowledge and skills. This chapter addresses four primary questions regarding technology in education: (a) What is the current state of K-12 mathematics instruction?

(b) What are the barriers to integrating technology with academic instruction? (c) Are today's classroom environments conducive to technology integration/infusion with instruction? and (d) Is there a practical model of technology infusion that maximizes both the efficiency of technology and the use of teacher expertise in the classroom?

Mathematics Instruction

The prominence of our nation's collective mathematical prowess is inextricably linked to its continued ability to develop and sustain new technology across many fields. The infusion of technology in business, education, health care, defense, and many other areas vital to our health as a nation is well documented. The National Mathematics Advisory Panel (2008) has identified a growing need for capable workers in the science and engineering workforce to replace a trend of accelerated retirements in the near future. In addition to sustaining our ability to staff the workforce in these vital areas, the panel cites the importance of mathematics education in providing pathways to college and career options. With the growth of mathematics-intensive science and engineering employment opportunities outpacing overall job growth by 3:1, the importance of mathematics proficiency for American students becomes critical to providing the expertise to fill these workforce needs.

Unfortunately, less than stellar performance by our nation's students casts serious doubt on our ability to develop this expertise on the scale that is needed. Less than one third of our eighth-grade students are proficient in mathematics, and less than one fourth are proficient at Grade 12 (National Mathematics Advisory Panel, 2008). In addition, racial/ethnic disparities have persisted over the last two decades despite incremental improvement in overall mathematics performance. Recent statistics reveal a 32-point gap in performance between White and Black eighth-grade students and a 26-point gap between White and Hispanic students (National Center for Education Statistics, 2009). Neither of these gaps is significantly different from those observed 20 years ago. Clearly, there is significant ground to be covered in order to ensure that all students are capable of better achievement patterns, and there is a particular need to address minority underperformance patterns that persist.

The National Mathematics Advisory Panel (2008) identified algebra as a central concern in addressing mathematics proficiency due to the sharp decline in U.S. student achievement in late middle school, when algebra coursework begins. Algebra proficiency is a strong predictor of college success as students who complete Algebra II are twice as likely to graduate from college compared with those that do not. Clearly, a focus on algebra can go a long way in improving our students' preparedness for both higher education as well as for science, technology, engineering, and mathematics (STEM)-related workforce opportunities. With so many students performing at below basic proficiency levels, any comprehensive approach must include component emphasizing development of the component skills necessary to be successful in algebra and higher mathematics. Technology can and probably will play an important role in this component due to the need for efficiency in assisting large numbers of students in becoming proficient at some basic skills.

Barriers to Technology Integration

Research on technology in the classroom suggests that wiring the schools to the Internet and installing computers in the classrooms are not enough to bring about integration of this technology into instructional practices. There are several common impediments to successful infusion, even after all of the hardware and software have been put into place. A review of 48 empirical studies from 1995 to 2006 examined barriers to integrating computers for instructional purposes in K-12 settings (Hew & Brush, 2007). The largest category of identified barriers was "resources," which included the amount of time needed to prepare technology-based lessons. It also included technical support to assist in using different technologies. A successful integration program can address these barriers by providing integration with existing curricula so that teachers don't have to invest time to prepare to use the technology. Also important is the level of onsite professional development addressing both technology-relevant pedagogical concerns and pedagogical content knowledge.

Another major barrier to K-12 technology integration is the effect of teacher attitudes and beliefs. Teacher decisions on whether to use computers to support instruction depend on the beliefs they hold about the potential benefits (or lack thereof) of computers to aid in the learning process (Ertmer, 2005). Zhao and Frank (2003) used an ecological metaphor to describe the introduction of computers into the classroom, identifying "ways of using computers" as an invading species and the teachers as a keystone species.

Technology uses that are simply duplications of the kinds of instruction that the teachers currently conduct can be viewed as a threat to the teacher and, thus, may be shunned or even subconsciously undermined. The fact that the classroom teacher controls all interactions between the student and the computer means that the teacher determines whether the "invading species" will survive. Programs that attempt to provide computer-based lessons, similar to those lessons that we might expect a teacher to conduct, fall into this category. Such virtual lessons may be better suited for distance learning or after-school programs, where they are not competing for the attention of the student with a living, breathing, decision-making teacher. In the classroom, computers will be better received by teachers if they are viewed as complementary to their lessons rather than competing forces. Such an approach could lead to a better learning experience, particularly if it focuses on relieving teachers of the burdens associated with routine practice exercises and proficiency management, allowing them more time to concentrate on guiding students to deeper conceptual understanding of content.

As for the teacher's beliefs about the benefits of using computers in instruction, providing content-focused professional development can help. Hew and Brush (2007) recommend making efforts to change teacher attitudes and beliefs about the potential for the use of computers in instruction. One way to accomplish this is to provide teachers with immediate data that they can use to make instructional decisions, along with training on how to use the data to shape ongoing instruction. An administrative component to software that provides class-level data in real time can provide a dynamic that traditional teaching methods cannot. This would give the teacher information that can be used immediately to determine whether difficulties are due to insufficient underlying skill development or to some other factor, such as lack of motivation or conceptual misunderstandings.

Motivational factors can be barriers to successful integration of computers in the classroom as well. Programs directed toward improving curriculum design while ignoring the motivational factors that contribute to underperformance may not be sufficient to tip the performance scales in a positive direction. The reciprocal nature of learning and motivation suggests that they must be addressed simultaneously. Motivation influences a person's approach to learning, whereas the learning that does occur influences the learner's motivation (Pintrich & Schunk, 2002). Therefore, student and teacher feedback is critical to smooth implementation of an innovative approach to instructional design. Student participation in the feedback loop can enhance their motivation as it engages them as a contributor to the learning process rather than an object of it.

Student motivation can also be influenced by the content-related feedback they receive when working with technology-based curricula. Immediate feedback is key to sustained engagement, allowing the students to know whether they are on the right track or need to adjust their thinking about a particular task. The tracking of prior performances also contributes to efforts to sustain student motivation as they work with the technology over time. Prior performance is the most reliable indicator used to assess self-efficacy (Bandura, 1986); therefore, timely and accurate feedback is critical to the development of positive self-efficacy beliefs.

A program designed to give immediate and continuous feedback to students will both remind them of their past successes and shape goal setting for current and future activity. Efficacy beliefs can also be molded or altered through effective observational modeling (Bandura & Locke, 2003). Observing successful models can lead to the belief that one can be successful as well (Schunk & Zimmerman, 2007; Zimmerman, 2000). This is where multimedia can be utilized to provide models of successful students, perhaps in the form of online video, to provide opportunities to learn from students in similar zones of proximal development. Video vignettes of diverse individuals in the STEM workforce discussing the importance of algebra to their success in life would serve to both teach and motivate.

Are Classrooms Ready?

Are current classroom environments conducive to effective technology implementation? At the present time, teachers by and large determine how their respective classroom activities are conducted. This can present a serious dilemma when we consider its possible ramifications to the implementation of technology in the classroom. Clark (2001) describes how a computer-based instruction (CBI) teacher may consciously or unconsciously reduce the learning impact of new technology when it is perceived as a threat to his or her job. One has to wonder whether a teacher's self-worth is vulnerable to an instrument that never gets sick, asks for a raise, or gets in a bad mood. How committed is the average teacher to ensuring that the computer assume some of the responsibility for student learning? This can create a conflict of interest due to the fact that the teacher must mediate the exchange between students and computers. It can also result in a potential confounding variable for any classroom-based research that compares computer-based instruction to traditional teaching methods.

Some question whether our nation's teachers are trained well enough to use technology as an effective tool for instruction. A National Center for Education Statistics (NCES) report reveals that, although better than 85% of our nation's public school districts *offer* teacher professional development in using multimedia content, specific software tools, and Internet resources for instruction, less than 17% of districts *require* teachers to receive professional development in any of these areas. Just 39% of public districts require that teachers receive professional development in integrating technology into instruction (Gray & Lewis, 2009).

Despite huge investments in technology infrastructure and equipment, the current state of classroom-level availability is hardly enough to support sustained class-level usage in most settings. If we aren't prepared to make computers readily available for entire classrooms of students as a common practice, one has to wonder how significant a factor computer use can be in affecting student performance outcomes overall.

NCES statistics indicate that, although technology availability is vastly improved from what it was a few decades ago, its effectiveness will not be measured in terms of improvement but rather will be determined by how sufficient it is to meaningfully integrate into daily instruction. The fact that 84% of the nation's public school teachers reported having at least one computer in their classroom for teacher activities is laudable, but this is not sufficient to support regular, classwide use of computer-based curricula. Thirty-six percent of teachers reported having *exactly* one computer in their class; 38% reported having between two and five computers, and only 10% reported having more than five computers (Gray & Lewis, 2009). With average class sizes continuing to increase, meaningful individual computer use in classrooms can be a scheduling and logistical nightmare. The challenges associated with rotating a class of 30 or more students through five or fewer computers, all while balancing concurrent activities for those not using the computers at any given time and dealing with other classroom management demands, can be quite overwhelming.

Even if there were general consensus that individual proficiency with computer-based content is a goal for 21st-century classrooms, what are the basic prerequisites for a student becoming an effective computer user? This will likely vary depending on the content and demands associated with a particular subject area and with specific types of software. Programs designed to address language arts content may be more demanding on keyboarding skills, which we cannot assume are necessarily a strength of the so-called "generation M^2" population despite their ever-increasing appetite for technology-based media. Some recent data indicate that, although computer use is at an all-time high for these media-savvy 8- to 18-year-olds, their computer use is primarily dominated by entertainment rather than academic demands. A recent national survey indicates that only one third of students in this age range report using a computer for school-related work on a typical day, and the average amount of time spent doing that school-related work was just 16 minutes (Rideout, Foehr, & Roberts, 2010).

An alternative to making keyboarding a required subject for all students would be to design instructional software that is less dependent on this skill. We sit students in front of computers as early as elementary school expecting them to use the keyboard and mouse to effectively interact with various software programs. Programs that require substantial textual responses clearly present an additional hurdle for students who must resort to "hunt and peck" strategies to respond. Software can eliminate much of this barrier by making the interaction by the student mouse driven as much as possible, or with touch screens, touch driven to the extent feasible. Despite the current low levels of computer use for school work, we can reasonably assume that most students are comfortable on some level with interacting with the computer using a mouse or other pointing device. In 2009, more than 90% of 8- to 18-year-olds surveyed reported having a computer in their homes. Sixty-four percent of this group reported using the home computer an average of more than 2 hours daily for recreational uses (i.e., social networking, watching videos, downloading music, etc.) (Rideout et al., 2010). Leveraging the skill set associated with these activities in the classroom can reduce the learning curve associated with a new learning program, provided the program can be designed so that novel user interface characteristics are kept to a minimum. Is there a practical model of technology infusion that maximizes both the efficiency of technology and the use of teacher expertise in the classroom? It seems that the computer "revolution" in education began and subsequently gained enormous steam before a clear-cut answer to an important question was determined: Is it our goal to put a computer in front of every child in a classroom? If so, it is important to know whether this goal is based on hard data on learning outcomes rather than perceived motivational benefits. It appears that we are eagerly treading down a path without a clear vision of what our destination will look like. Before we can do meaningful research as to the potential effect of computers in the classroom, don't we have to have a model of what full implementation looks like? If full implementation means a computer at every desk, students prepared to use them, and teachers eager (or at least willing) to incorporate them to the fullest extent possible, then I ask, where are the models of this vision?

If we could instantly put enough computers in every classroom to allow for one-to-one computer access for all of the nations' students, would we expect to subsequently see evidence of increased learning? If so, how long would it take? The path that the business community took to incorporate technology may provide some answers to these questions. Short-term research on the effects of technology on production found positive correlation difficult to quantify. However, long-term analyses were much more successful in this regard. Research by Brynjolfsson and Hitt (2003) explored the relationship between computers and productivity by examining data from more than 500 large U.S. firms from 1987 to 1994. They suggest that, due to the adjustment time and learning curve associated with the computerization of workplaces, productivity and output benefits derived from such computerization are up to five times greater when viewed over 5- to 7-year spans as compared with 1-year returns, partly due to the need to include complementary investments in work practices, human capital, and firm restructuring (Brynjolfsson & Hitt, 2003).

Given the current state of the average American classroom, one would be hard pressed to conclude that anything close to the complementary investments in work practices, human capital, or restructuring has occurred. If we in fact want to utilize the computer as a medium to foster individual learning, then we must change the work practices at the classroom level to facilitate this change. This means overcoming the opposition that teachers might present. It also means reexamining some of the methods that we have been using to deliver instruction for more than 100 years. Perhaps most important, it means committing the resources required to ensure that an individual computing model becomes a reality in the classroom.

However, if it is not the intent to put computing power in the hands of each individual student, then we must reexamine our notion of what computers will do for education. If full-scale implementation is not the goal, then we should treat computers as just another tool to enhance the way we prepare for and administer lessons, rather than a revolutionary tool that will change the way instruction is delivered in a systematic way. Our investment as a nation in technology in educational settings suggests that we believe technology to be potentially transformative and beneficial at the individual student level. However, the lack of any kind of consensus on how this is accomplished means that more research is necessary before we can discern which approaches will bring the hoped-for transformation in effective and efficient ways. This study examines one approach wherein the computer can be harnessed to assist in the learning process and in the delivery of fundamental content in mathematics.

Classroom Technology Integration Study

Computer-Based Math Concept Acquisition and Automaticity

In this study, the effects of distributed practice on an array of math concepts were examined. Seventh graders practiced math skills 3 days per week, 10 minutes per day, using a game-based computer program designed to establish and strengthen their automatic recall of 10 different math skills. These skills are foundational for complex problem solving. The computer-based program included 1-minute drills on math skills, combined with categorization tasks to facilitate schema acquisition rather than simple rote memorization. Significant increases in the overall number of items attempted and the percentage of correct responses were observed. In addition, significant decreases were observed in the average item response time for the individual skills practiced. Implications for schema development and automaticity of constituent math skills are discussed, as well as the impact that this technology-aided approach can have on content knowledge acquisition.

Objective/Purpose

The role of working memory as a significant factor in the performance of complex cognitive tasks, particularly those related to academic achievement and intelligence, has been well documented (Conway, Kane, & Engle, 2003; Engle, Tuholski, Laughlin, & Conway, 1999; Gathercole & Pickering, 2000;

Gathercole, Pickering, Knight, & Stegmann, 2004; Kyllonen & Christal, 1990). Cognitive load theorists posit that working memory limitations exist, but experts are able to augment working memory through the automation of subcomponents used in problem solving. They are able to handle many components of complex problems by developing efficient schemata or mental patterns, which combine simpler elements into more manageable conceptual understanding (van Merrienboer & Sweller, 2005).

Although our aim as educators is not to make every student an "expert" in algebra or any of the other subjects we teach, we can apply the principles of expert cognitive load management to areas of complexity that exist within our curricula. In algebra, students must learn to mentally access and manipulate basic mathematical skills, algebraic concepts, and complex formulas to assist in problem-solving tasks. This task becomes much easier when basic foundational skills are learned to automaticity, such that mental resources can be preserved to assist in grasping the big picture rather than consumed by the processing of minute procedural details. This is where computers can contribute greatly to the proficiency of students who have difficulty due to their insufficient foundational skills. Compter-Based Instruction has been demonstrated to be an effective tool in helping struggling K-12 students to fare better on annual standardized math assessments (Hannafin & Foshay, 2008). The purpose of this work was to facilitate the systematic acquisition of conceptual understanding of mathematics by blending skill practice with schema acquisition using a computer-based model. The combination of well-organized schemata and an improved level of automaticity on constituent skills will allow students to handle more complex problem solving by freeing up working memory resources to devote to novel solutions.

Theoretical Framework

Several models of memory have been conceptualized to represent the presumed components of memory. Many prominent models include a three-store system comprised of sensory memory, working memory, and long-term memory (Miyake & Shah, 1999). The working memory component has been described as the resource responsible for holding and processing information that one is consciously attending to (Baddeley, 2006; Baddeley & Hitch, 1974). Whereas researchers may disagree on the structure of memory or its effects on the recall of different types of information, working memory is widely regarded as a limited resource. Nonetheless, there are examples of expertise wherein individuals are able to mentally process and manipulate large amounts of information concurrently—amounts that far exceed the presumed limits of working memory.

Research on expertise suggests that traditional models of working memory cannot account for the extended amounts of complex information that are readily accessible to experts who have honed their expertise over many years. The acquisition of expertise generally follows a pattern in which many cognitive components of a domain are "overlearned" to the extent that they become automated knowledge, requiring little, if any, of the controlled processing that places heavy demands on working memory. The fact that experts have large amounts of readily accessible information might suggest that they have increased their working memory capacity. However, the fact that such increased capacity is available *only* in their respective domains of expertise suggests that long-term memory is involved. Well-learned patterns of information processing increase experts' abilities to process more and more information, but it is the stable mental representations in long-term memory, or schemata, that are presumed to be the means by which large amounts of information can be handled so efficiently (Ericsson & Kintsch, 1995). By facilitating the acquisition of automaticity and rich content schemata, educators can move students toward greater levels of expertise in mathematics.

Methods

Participants

Forty-nine seventh-grade students from two pre-algebra classes participated in the study. The study was conducted at a Southern California intermediate school that has a student population consisting of approximately 650 seventh and eighth graders only. The school is part of a small district that serves approximately 4,700 students. The district is located about 45 minutes outside of a large metropolitan city and has a student population comprised of 71% Latino, 9% African American, 9% White, and 11% other races. Of the 49 participants in this study, 21 were male and 28 female. There were 40 Latino, four African American, four White, and one Filipino participant(s).

Instrumentation and Procedure

Two seventh-grade pre-algebra classes from one of the two seventh-grade math teachers were randomly selected to participate in the study. Institutional Review Board and parental permission were obtained for all participating students. This chapter reports on the third phase of a series of computer-based interventions with the same classes. The first two phases examined simple recall of numeric and alphanumeric character strings (Howard, 2009). In this, the third and final phase, participants completed a series of 10 one-minute drills on math concepts that are assessed annually, either directly or indirectly, on the seventh-grade California Standardized Test in mathematics. The 10 drills addressed the following concepts: scientific notation, integer exponents, fractional exponents, rational number equivalence, square roots, absolute value, basic operations ($+$, $-$, x, $\div$) with integers, basic operations with fractions, slope, and properties of linear equations.

The set of 10 drills were presented to the students in the form of a PC computer program developed specifically for this study. Participants were given two practice sessions on two separate days prior to data collection to familiarize themselves with the program and the concepts being covered on the drills. Prior to each 1-minute drill, the name of the concept being drilled appeared at the top of the response area on the computer screen. An on-screen timer informed the user of the time left on each drill. After the drill time had elapsed, the user was cued to identify the mathematical category for the just completed drill. This element was intended to help the user connect each drill to its respective mathematical language to facilitate better schema development. The program awarded points to participants for accuracy and speed in completing the math skill drills, and it provided them with hints on completing the problems they had difficulty with if requested. The participants were also awarded points for speed and accuracy in identifying the categories.

Data Sources

Participant data were collected by the program and saved to a database—a process that was transparent to the user. These data included the number of attempted items, percentage correct, and average response times for individual drills. The students participated in the drills for five sessions over a 9-day period. The sessions were conducted during the first 10 to 15 minutes of their class period, followed by their regularly scheduled math lessons.

One-way repeated measures, analyses of variance (ANOVAs) were conducted to compare participant speed and accuracy over four points of measurement. The sessions occurred during the last 2 weeks of the school year, after the grades had been submitted, so there were significant numbers of absent students. Therefore, this analysis only included students who were present for at least four points of measurement ($n = 40$). The results for overall attempts and accuracy are reported below as well as average response time and accuracy for 3 of the 10 drills. Similar results were observed across the array of drills.

Results

One-way repeated measures (ANOVAs) were conducted to compare the overall number of attempts and percentages correct, as measured at four times over the 9-day intervention period, covering the full array of 10-component math skill drills. The means and standard deviations are presented in Table 7.1. There was a significant effect for time on the total number of items attempted [Wilks' Lambda $= .56$, $F(3, 37) = 9.90$, $p < .0005$, multivariate partial beta squared $= .45$]. There was also a significant effect for time on the overall percentage of correct responses over the 10 drills [Wilks' Lambda $= .53$, $F(3, 37) = 10.81$, $p < .0005$, multivariate partial beta squared $= .47$].

Table 7.1: Descriptive Statistics for Overall Attempts and Percentage Correct ($n = 40$)

Time Period	No. of Attempts		Percentage Correct	
	Mean	SD	Mean	SD
Time 1	140.90	30.22	72.67	17.29
Time 2	151.13	37.59	75.75	16.71
Time 3	156.87	37.23	77.95	14.84
Time 4	164.88	40.27	80.03	14.97

One-way repeated measures (ANOVAs) were conducted to compare the average response time and percentages correct on the scientific notation drill over the four points of measurement. The means and standard deviations are presented in Table 7.2. There was a significant effect for time on average response time [Wilks' Lambda $= .63$, $F(3, 37) = 7.20$, $p = .001$, multivariate partial beta squared $= .37$]. There was also a significant effect for time on the percentage of correct responses on the scientific notation drill [Wilks'

Lambda = .70, $F(3, 37)$ = 5.25, p = .004, multivariate partial beta squared = .30].

Table 7.2: Descriptive Statistics for Average Response Time and Percentage Correct on Scientific Notation Drill (n = 40)

Time Period	Avg. Response Time		Percentage Correct	
	Mean	SD	Mean	SD
Time 1	3.91	1.28	76.55	23.53
Time 2	3.32	.88	76.38	23.35
Time 3	3.22	.89	79.05	21.19
Time 4	3.33	1.30	85.13	18.92

One-way repeated measures (ANOVAs) were conducted to compare the average response time and percentages correct on the square roots drill over the four points of measurement. The means and standard deviations are presented in Table 7.3. There was a significant effect for time on average response time [Wilks' Lambda = .56, $F(3, 37)$ = 9.62, p < .0005, multivariate partial beta squared = .44]. There was not a significant effect for time on the percentage of correct responses on the square roots drill [Wilks' Lambda = .88, $F(3, 37)$ = 1.71, p = .181, multivariate partial beta squared = .12].

Table 7.3: Descriptive Statistics for Average Response Time and Percentage Correct on Square Roots Drill (n = 40)

Time Period	Avg. Response Time		Percentage Correct	
	Mean	SD	Mean	SD
Time 1	2.79	.76	83.80	20.81
Time 2	2.50	.65	85.85	17.98
Time 3	2.52	.84	86.35	18.74
Time 4	2.32	.63	88.20	16.02

One-way repeated measures (ANOVAs) were conducted to compare the average response time and percentages correct on the exponents drill over the four points of measurement. The means and standard deviations are presented in Table 7.4. There was a significant effect for time on average response time [Wilks' Lambda = .73, $F(3, 37)$ = 4.57, p = .008, multivariate partial beta squared = .27]. There was also a significant effect for time on the percentage of correct responses on the exponents drill [Wilks' Lambda = .81, $F(3, 37) = 2.90$, $p = .048$, multivariate partial beta squared = .19].

Table 7.4: Descriptive Statistics for Average Response Time and Percentage Correct on Exponents Drill ($n = 40$)

Time Period	Avg. Response Time		Percentage Correct	
	Mean	SD	Mean	SD
Time 1	2.89	.78	84.70	17.29
Time 2	2.90	1.04	88.32	11.94
Time 3	2.72	.88	91.20	10.87
Time 4	2.51	.77	90.77	11.93

Conclusion

This study represents a first step in demonstrating a feasible model of technology infusion in the classroom in such a way that it is aligned with the existing curriculum, nonthreatening to the teachers who are charged with implementing it, and supportive of efforts at helping students to take basic skills off of their working memory plate as they attempt more complex problem solving. By utilizing an administrative component of the software to provide real-time data to the teacher, the computer was implemented in such a way that it was an ally to the teacher's aims, not a replacement for good teaching in the classroom. This is an important issue during implementation because it helps to overcome any fears that teachers may have over the possibility of being replaced by computers.

As for student achievement, their use of the computer-based program for 10 to 15 minutes at the beginning of class two to three times per week resulted in the average response time on constituent math skills decreasing significantly, whereas accuracy was maintained or significantly increased over an array of important math skills. Faster response times on individual drills suggest an increase in automaticity in recall of skills needed to solve more complex problems. Expertise in a given field is directly influenced by the level of schemata acquired and the level of automaticity an individual has developed within the domain. An intervention that systematically facilitates both schema acquisition and automaticity can provide students with the expertise they need to successfully engage in more complex problem solving as demanded by higher mathematics.

The model employed in this study demonstrated that constituent math skills can be improved significantly in a short period of time by allowing individual students regular access to computers. The use of wireless laptops for each student in the class, along with a software program that provided the teacher with live data on student performance, created a glimpse of what is possible when we commit to allowing each student to harness the computing power that technology offers.

The current state of instruction in this country suggests that we could be doing a much better job of taking advantage of technology in the instruction of mathematics as well as other subjects. Many barriers have been identified that hinder attempts at technology infusion in K-12 education, but the existence of enormous technology resources in the nation's classrooms makes it an issue that cannot be ignored. The financial investment has been and continues to be made with the ever-elusive goal of improved academic achievement in sight. Practical models of integration and infusion, which take into consideration the affective and practical barriers that prevent technology use, can be a promising direction in education. Using technology in ways that improve necessary skills while improving teacher proficiency creates a "win-win" proposition for teachers and students. In such a scenario, perhaps we can finally reap the long-sought benefits of our investments of faith and finances in the promise of technology.

When President Obama articulated his vision of a classroom where each student has a laptop at his or her desk, we must assume that his vision included well-conceived plans on how those computers would be used to improve the academic outcomes for those students. If these modernized classrooms are to be successful, it is incumbent on educators and technology innovators to create the tools and pedagogy to ensure that the classroom technology is welcomed, utilized, and effective when called on to take education to greater heights. A research-driven approach to examine the feasibility and effectiveness of various approaches, such as the one utilized in this study, will help provide educators with confidence that the investments in technology can make the 21st-century classroom a reality.

References

Baddeley, A. (2006). Working memory: An overview. In S. J. Pickering (Ed.), *Working Memory and Education* (pp. 1–31). Amsterdam: Elsevier.

Baddeley, A., & Hitch, G. J. (1974). Working memory. *The psychology of learning and motivation: Advances in research and theory* (Vol. 8, pp. 47–89). New York: Academic Press.

Bandura, A. (1986). *Social foundations of thought and action: A social cognitive theory.* Englewood Cliffs, NJ: Prentice-Hall.

Bandura, A., & Locke, E. A. (2003). Negative self-efficacy and goal effects revisited. *Journal of Applied Psychology, 88*(1), 87–99.

Barack in Dayton: A new vision for a 21st century education. (2008). Retrieved May 24, 2010, from http://my.barackobama.com/page/community/post/amandascott/gG5pB4

Brynjolfsson, E., & Hitt, L. M. (2003). Computing productivity: Firm-level evidence. *Review of Economics and Statistics, 85*(4), 777–792.

Clark, R. E. (2001). *Learning from media: Arguments, analysis and evidence.* Greenwich, CT: Information Age Publishers.

Conway, A. R. A., Kane, M. J., & Engle, R. W. (2003). Working memory capacity and its relation to general intelligence. *Trends in Cognitive Sciences, 7*(12), 547–552.

Engle, R. W., Tuholski, S. W., Laughlin, J. E., & Conway, A. R. A. (1999). Working memory, short-term memory, and general fluid intelligence: A latent-variable approach. *Journal of Experimental Psychology, 128*(3), 309–331.

Ericsson, K. A., & Kintsch, W. (1995). Long-term working-memory. *Psychological Review, 102*(2), 211–245.

Ertmer, P. A. (2005). Teacher pedagogical beliefs: The final frontier in our quest for technology integration? *Educational Technology, Research and Development, 53*, 25–39.

Fletcher, G. H. (2010). Was I wrong on Obama? *T.H.E. Journal, 37*(3), 10, 12–13.

Gathercole, S. E., & Pickering, S. J. (2000). Working memory deficits in children with low achievements in the national curriculum at 7 years of age. *British Journal of Educational Psychology, 70*, 177–194.

Gathercole, S. E., Pickering, S. J., Knight, C., & Stegmann, Z. (2004). Working memory skills and educational attainment: Evidence from National Curriculum Assessments at 7 and 14 years of age. *Applied Cognitive Psychology, 18*, 1–16.

Gray, L., & Lewis, L. (2009). *Educational technology in public school districts: Fall 2008* (NCES 2010–003). Washington, DC: National Center for Education Statistics, Institute of Education Sciences, U.S. Department of Education.

Hannafin, R. D., & Foshay, W. R. (2008). Computer-based instruction's (CBI) rediscovered role in K-12: An evaluation case study of one high school's use of CBI to improve pass rates on high-stakes tests. *Educational Technology, Research and Development, 56*(2), 147–160.

Hew, K. F., & Brush, T. (2007). Integrating technology into k-12 teaching and learning: Current knowledge gaps and recommendations for future research. *Educational Technology, Research and Development, 55*, 223–252.

Howard, K. (2009). *Transfer effects of working memory capacity.* Paper presented at the American Educational Research Association, San Diego, CA.

Kyllonen, P. C., & Christal, R. E. (1990). Reasoning ability is (little more than) working-memory capacity?! *Intelligence, 14*, 389–433.

Miyake, A., & Shah, P. (Eds.). (1999). *Models of working memory: Mechanisms of active maintenance and executive control.* New York: Cambridge University Press.

National Center for Education Statistics. (2009). *The nation's report card: Mathematics 2009* (NCES 2010-451). Washington, DC: U.S. Department of Education, Institute of Education Sciences.

National Mathematics Advisory Panel. (2008). *Foundations for success: The final report of the National Mathematics Advisory Panel.* Washington, DC: U.S. Department of Education.

Pintrich, P. R., & Schunk, D. H. (2002). *Motivation in education* (2nd ed.). Upper Saddle River, NJ: Merrill Prentice-Hall.

Rideout, V. J., Foehr, U. G., & Roberts, D. F. (2010). *Generation M^2: Media in the lives of 8- to 18-year-olds.* Menlo Park, CA: Henry J. Kaiser Family Foundation.

Schunk, D. H., & Zimmerman, B. J. (2007). Influencing children's self-efficacy and self-regulation of reading and writing through modeling. *Reading & Writing Quarterly, 23*, 7–25.

van Merrienboer, J. J. G., & Sweller, J. (2005). Cognitive load theory and complex learning: Recent developments and future directions. *Educational Psychology Review, 17*(2), 147–177.

Zhao, Y., & Frank, K. A. (2003). Factors affecting technology uses in schools: An ecological perspective. *American Educational Research Journal, 40*(4), 807–840.

Zimmerman, B. J. (2000). Self-efficacy: An essential motive to learn. *Contemporary Educational Psychology, 25*, 82–91.

The Hope for Audacity: Moving from Adversarial Contests to Respectful Alliances

Alice H. Merz & Terri Jo Swim

This book began with the audacious hope that President Obama would signal the start of a new era in education. We anticipated that he would take a different direction than past presidents, who saw children, teachers, and schools as just test scores or failures. From his autobiographies and campaign speeches, we believed that Mr. Obama understood the impact that he and others can have in helping to positively shape children's education and future. We believed that he understood that it was not a black-and-white issue but one of complexity that needed someone of intellect and integrity who could lead our education in a better direction. As the title of this book indicates, we still hope for some audacity and courage from our president and others to lead us in the right race in our children's education.

After Mr. Obama won the election, we were even more hopeful. When his appointment for Secretary of Education narrowed to Linda Darling-Hammond and Arne Duncan, we were proud that President Obama considered Dr. Darling-Hammond, a person who has demonstrated over and over her ability to be a leader who can make a difference. We believed that with President Obama and Dr. Darling-Hammond at the helm of our nation's education, the profession would be elevated to one of respect and increased quality.

When Mr. Duncan was appointed, we found discourses instead congealing around the idea of how bad teachers are. It became about getting rid of teachers. It became about short-cutting or short-circuiting teacher preparation with abbreviated programs or lessening licensure requirements (Chea, 2011) as a way to get higher-quality teachers into the classroom. It became about merit pay, which led to behind-the-scenes discussions about which teachers get which special needs children because those children's scores will either raise or lower teachers' pay. It continued the one-size-fits-all approach and drive for identical outcomes, with no differentiation for our students with special needs, such as those learning a new language, those who are gifted, or those with learning difficulties. The discourse also moved to include talk about competitions for funding that provoked states, like Indiana, to coerce teachers to give up many things in order to receive money for the children's education, with little guarantee that they would even receive the money needed.

These sample discourses found in the media were even heard and discussed at home by Alice's children. What follows is a brief overview of those conversations.

My son, who is 10 years old, loves mathematics and is good at it. For a long time now, he has said that he wants to be a math teacher. He has enjoyed his teachers and how they have tried to further his abilities in math as well as other subject areas. As his parents, my husband and I are glad that he sees teaching as a valuable profession. We are also pleased with his interest in mathematics because it is an important field in the global economy, as well as an important tool that is used in a number of other professions.

This year, my son has become interested in how people think about teachers and other professions. He was shocked that teachers are not valued money-wise (i.e., salary-wise). He also learned from the media, noneducators, and even the president that people are verbally disrespectful of teachers; he found that they were stating over and over how bad teachers are. My son says that now he doesn't want to teach; he doesn't want to be disrespected. Who does?

You see, at my son's school, the teachers work hard at having the children respect one another. They learn that incivilities tend to tear down a community rather than build it up, let alone the fact that no one deserves to be disrespected or bullied. For my son, it felt like a contradiction between what they were learning at school and the rhetoric that was being modelled outside the school walls.

So, it provokes the questions: Is this what society and the president, via Arne Duncan, wanted to do to improve education and our pool of quality teachers? What may be more helpful?

While Alice's son, teachers, and others have felt or been the recipient of the negativity from the incivilities of these discourses, the point that politicians need to hear is that finger-pointing, bullying, and blame will not solve the problem. Although politicians tend to compete for people's attention with incivilities, the process does not build trust (Mutz & Reeves, 2005). Making people feel bad only distracts from what needs to be done and exacerbates the incivility. Seita and Brendtro (2003) explain that within these kinds of adversarial contests, there are feelings and behaviors associated with distrust, antagonism, and detachment that will move people further away from a common goal.

As parents, when our children start to feel that strongly about something they don't like, we occasionally suggests that they turn it around and ask, "How may I help? What is something we can agree on? What goals do we each have? How can we both reach a part of our goal?" According to Mr. Obama, his mother understood empathy when she would ask him, "How do you think that would feel?" (Obama, 2006, p. 80). According to Seita and Brendtro (2003), the recommendation for turning "adversarial relations" around is to find ways to build "respectful alliances" or ways of working together with civility that lead to opportunities for trust, collaboration, and attachment.

In this book, the authors pooled their expertise and collaborated to provide some meaningful information for the president, Mr. Duncan, and others interested in educational policies and practices. We realize that noneducators may not be familiar with what is working in education if they are only hearing or paying attention to the rhetoric from politicians or journalists. Although politicians move in circles of adversarial relations and contests, the authors in this book align more with developing respectful alliances. Because this may be unfamiliar, it is the authors' goal to note the familiar and then provide alternatives for reaching the goal of supporting children's learning. We believe that by providing more information, we can work with politicians and the reader to build alliances that will make our educational system better for the children. We believe that everyone can agree that it is important that children are learning to the best of their ability, and we recognize that there have been multiple approaches and policies that have tried to make this happen. The question that remains, and which is addressed, is how can we work together in a civil manner that breeds trust, support, and more progress?

In each chapter, the threads of the civility continuum were found occurring in multiple layers in society (i.e., in the politicians' layer, the public community layer, the teachers' layer, the parents' layer, or the children's layer). Each chapter addressed some of these layers and provided more guidance for moving toward or maintaining civility, a robust hope, and rich learning in education. Although the authors in this book do not specifically use the term civility in their chapters, they allude to different ideas along the civility continuum that will be brought out in this chapter. At the top of the civility spectrum, they talked about respect; a valuing of children, rich learning, and teaching; and ultimately people working together with trust. At the lower end of the civility spectrum, they talked about the need to move away from incivility because it breeds rudeness, disrespect, and a lack of trust and because it moves people into adversarial relations, working at cross-purposes, bullying, or coercion.

Kanpol, Strople, and Leatherman and her colleagues all addressed incivilities in the political layer, albeit from slightly diverse perspectives and by connecting consequences for different layers. Kanpol (Introduction) viewed incivility as the deskilling of teachers' capabilities through political mandates or impositions. These mandates often require teachers to implement trivial rules that do not get at the important aspects of teaching and that detach teachers from the complex and expert decision making that is inherent in meaningful teaching. Leatherman, Bangel, Cox, Merrill, and Newsome (Chapter 5) paralleled this idea when they expanded the conversation to include the political mandate for teacher collaboration. When teachers collaborate in superficial ways to just meet the "letter of the law," a contrived collaboration results between teachers that is "not voluntary and spontaneous…[where] implementation is the focus rather than [professional] development" (Pine, 2009, p. 156). The authors imply that when the teachers align with the policy level, they inadvertently set up an adversarial relationship between themselves and other layers because it becomes extremely difficult to meet the needs of special needs children. Similarly, Strople (Chapter 1) raised for discussion the consequences of teachers and children being defined as successful or not by standardized tests that assess the limited subjects of language arts and mathematics. Under these conditions, feelings of incivility occur when certain school subjects, certain children, and certain cultures become marginalized. All three chapters explored how adversarial contests between teacher and student, teacher against teacher, teacher against cultures, and teachers against policies or policymakers resulted from educational policies that deskilled teachers, mandated collaboration, or limited assessments of performance. When people at various layers begin to work at cross purposes, the original value of education and caring for students becomes obfuscated or lost. We must move beyond political finger pointing and move the profession forward through alliances that involve authentic collaborations and cooperation between layers and within each layer.

Isik-Ercan and Howard shifted the readers' focus from a primary emphasis on policy to stressing civility at the layer of teachers. Isik-Ercan (Chapter 4) pointed out that teachers often view reform policies as adversarial because the mandates are minimally based on research, rarely are built in collaboration with teachers, and neglect the complexity of variables that are inherent in teaching. In order for reform efforts to be more effective, Isik-Ercan articulated a need for civility based on trust that crosses multiple layers. Teachers need to collaborate with each other and policymakers need to trust and collaborate with teachers. In Swim's terms (Chapter 3), teachers need to be seen as rich, capable resources. By teachers being an active part of the reform efforts and receiving the necessary support, they can feel ownership, have a vision, and experience the growth that the new ideas can provoke in themselves and their students. Howard (Chapter 7) used the example of teachers using technology as a tool for creating alliances among each other, students, parents, and community members (e.g., businesses). Because of the emphasis placed on technology within our society, he wanted teachers to harness the powers of the tool for teaching. Technology was used to provide timely feedback regarding the children's learning, so that the teachers could appropriately tailor instruction to meet the needs of individual adolescents. According to these authors, when teachers gain more voice and work together through their differences toward new professional knowledge and, ultimately, better classroom practices, they will transform teaching from "an isolated activity into a foundation for school success" (Isik-Ercan, Chapter 4).

Three other chapters in the book, while recognizing important facets of the layers of policy, teachers, and community, emphasize civility at the layer of the child. Swim, Kim, and Mardell and his colleagues all discuss pathways for building higher quality classrooms. Swim (Chapter 3) and Mardell, Fiore, Boni, and Tonachel (Chapter 2) viewed civilities as being centered around seeing and treating all learners as rich resources with many capabilities, which is in opposition to the incivilities that result when people treat learners as needy and as having limited capability. Mardell et al. (Chapter 2) extended beyond the distinction between how one sees the learners (i.e., as rich or needy) to explore the rights of young children and teachers. These authors believe that recognizing and listening to the children, providing opportunities for them to learn through play, and providing meaningful and reasonable instruction and evaluations of their learning and growth are rights they must be afforded in a quality education system.

Kim (Chapter 6) noted that a teacher's choice of instruction can build alliances or adversarial contests with students depending on the approach. A recitation approach to teaching literacy involves a student building an alliance with the teacher and possibly an adversarial contest with other students (or even the teacher). In contrast, a critical thinking approach to teaching encourages the children to build alliances with each other to the benefit of all involved. The process builds trust and collaborative efforts among the children when they work together to find a viable solution, not just a particular "right" answer. Civility is developed as the children learn to think about alternative perspectives and options rather than just arguing their own point. All three of these chapters illustrated strategies for helping teachers and others develop the ability to see and assess the children as rich, capable thinkers. In addition, the strategies employed were not just of immediate benefit, they hold long-term benefits as well. When teachers come to see and treat the children as rich resources, they promote civility, trust, and meaningful alliances that could include teacher educators, prospective teachers, and the children. Furthermore, Kim implied that changes in the civility culture may be developed in future generations of children, who then can carry it into adulthood when meaningful opportunities are provided. Because teachers play such critical roles in whether they engage some or all children in rich learning opportunities, it can be inferred from these chapters that it is important to not distract the teachers with mandates that can take away the flexibility needed to accomplish this type of work with children.

In conclusion, the hope for audacious change was clearly articulated by each author in this book, pinpointing possibilities for building alliances and civilities that undergird solid educational policies and ultimately benefit teachers and children. There is one thing that we are sure about regarding our educational system: We are expecting more from it. If we want our children to have more skills and to participate successfully in a changing world, everyone else in the system has to increase their knowledge, skills, and dispositions. Legislators, teachers, parents, and administrators will have to grow in expertise, and it will not be easy or painless for anyone. Systematic change requires hope, audacious visions, hard work, and the courage to make bold changes. As outlined in this book, it takes courage

- for teachers to relax union work rules;
- to value multiple cultures;
- for parents to become better informed about their children's education, to make informed decisions about what kind of school their child attends, and to determine whether it is doing enough to meet their children's needs;
- for teachers to be reskilled and have freedom to use their expertise to build alliances that personalize and individualize the curriculum to meet each child's needs;
- for school principals to work with their teachers to improve their skills;
- for legislatures to relax the mandates, eschew the simple sound bites, increase their knowledge of the complexities of education, and embrace the findings of educational researchers;
- for professors of education to tackle the hard work of explaining complex facets of education to all parties; and
- to work together to improve our educational system.

If teachers and students are encouraged to be bold in their problem solving rather than deskilled and seen as needy or "bad," they will find ways to make the audacious changes that we all desire. Although this chapter has promoted respectful alliances as opposed to adversarial relations (Seita & Brendtro, 2003), it is understood that even with alliances, there will be confrontations when new ideas bump into old ideas or when different perspectives bump into each other (Isik-Ercan, Chapter 4; Pine, 2009). What is important, however, is to approach the process as critical, collaborative thinkers who are willing to examine different ways of thinking in order to come up with a solution (Kim, Chapter 6) and to ensure that "people are valued and respected" (Pine, 2009, p. 157) along the way.

This takes civility. As we gather hope and courage to make our own audacious changes, we also have to be supportive of each other while we experience the complexities and struggles of growing, learning about new perspectives, and changing. We have to ask each other, "How can we work together, even when we bump into each other's ideas? How can we help each other?" According to Obama (2006),

That's what empathy does—it calls us all to task....We are all shaken out of our complacency. We are all forced beyond our limited vision. No one is exempt from the call to find common ground. Of course, in the end a sense of mutual understanding isn't enough. After all, talk is cheap; like any value, empathy must be acted upon. (pp. 82–83)

So, let's be audacious. Let's move from demoralizing and deskilling teachers to supporting them. Let's move from seeing teachers and children as needy to seeing them as rich resources. Let's move from children learning just through recitation to becoming critical thinkers. Let's move from defending our own limited position with mandates to building a system that can grow and expand into a new realm of possibilities. It is simple to make these statements, yet the complexity that is required to do this at multiple layers makes systematic change extremely challenging. If we can raise the status of the teaching profession through civility and if we can build empathic alliances, then bright individuals like Alice's son will be interested again in the teaching profession.

References

Chea, T. (2011, January 4). New law labels interns "highly qualified teachers." *The Washington Post*. Available at http://www.washingtonpost.com/wp-yn/content/article/2011/01/04/AR2011010403334.html

Mutz, D. C., & Reeves, B. (2005). The new videomalaise: Effects of televised incivility on political trust. *The American Political Science Review*, 99(1), 1–15.

Obama, B. (2006). *The audacity of hope: Thoughts on reclaiming the American dream.* New York: Vintage Books.

Pine, G. J. (2009). *Teacher action research: Building knowledge democracies.* Los Angeles: Sage.

Seita, J. R., & Brendtro, L. K. (2003). Adversarial contests or respectful alliances. *Reclaiming Children and Youth*, 12(1), 58–60.

About the Authors

Nancy J. Bangel, Ph.D., earned her degrees in Gifted Education from Purdue University, West Lafayette, Indiana. Her research interests include techniques for enhancing the preservice teacher's knowledge of gifted students, gifted females, and gifted students' views of giftedness. Her articles have been published in *Gifted Child Quarterly*; *Journal for the Education of the Gifted*; *Understanding Our Gifted*; and the *Encyclopedia of Giftedness, Creativity, and Talent*. She has presented research findings concerning gifted students and the preservice teacher's knowledge of giftedness at national, regional, state, and local conferences as well as working with parent groups to understand their children's needs and how to advocate for their children.

Marina Boni has been involved in Early Childhood Education for the last 25 years. She is now working as mentor/coach in the Department of Early Childhood of the Boston Public Schools (BPS). Most of her work is about supporting teachers and schools as they go through the NAEYC accreditation process. She also facilitates professional development for the teachers specifically around Making Learning Visible and inspiration from the pre-primary schools in Reggio Emilia, Italy. Before coming to BPS Marina taught 3-to 5-year-olds at the Cambridgeport Children Center for 20 years.

Tracy Cox received her bachelor of arts in Education from Purdue University and her master of arts in Reading from Indiana University-Purdue University Fort Wayne. She has been an elementary classroom teacher as well as a reading specialist for her school district for 18 years. She has received numerous accolades for her work with elementary students, particularly focusing on her ability to advance the young student's reading ability.

Lisa Fiore is dean of faculty and an associate professor of Early Childhood Education at Lesley University. She received her doctorate in Developmental and Educational Psychology from Boston College and is the author of several books, including *Assessment of Young Children: A Collaborative Approach* and *Lifesmart: Exploring Human Development*. Her current research interests include early childhood assessment and documentation, and collaborating with practitioners to discuss and apply ideas inspired by the Reggio Emilia approach to early childhood education.

Keith Howard previously worked as a mathematics teacher, computer science teacher, and a technology coordinator in the Los Angeles Unified School District. He received his Ph.D. in Educational Psychology and Technology at the University of Southern California. He has taught courses in Educational Psychology at USC, UCLA, and CSUDH, as well as courses in Educational Technology at Chapman University. He is currently an assistant professor and coordinator of secondary education at Chapman University, where he serves as the inaugural director of the Donna Ford Attallah Academy for Teaching and Learning.

Zeynep Isik-Ercan is an assistant professor in Early Childhood Education at Indiana University-Purdue University Fort Wayne. She earned her doctoral degree in Early Childhood and Elementary Education from The Ohio State University. She teaches courses on pedagogy, families, curriculum, and theories of development and learning in early childhood and elementary education. Her research focuses on social contexts of education and cultural diversity, particularly educational experiences of culturally and linguistically diverse children and immigrants, and teacher growth to address the challenges of these contexts. Her most recent research projects include the use of 3D technologies for science and literacy learning in linguistically diverse second grade classrooms and refugee families' experiences with schooling.

Barry Kanpol is the current dean of the College of Education and Public Policy at Indiana University-Purdue University Fort Wayne. He obtained his Ph.D. from The Ohio State University. He has authored or co-authored 11 books and written over 70 articles and book chapters. His research interests center on critical issues in education—race, class, gender, urban concerns and popular culture. His current interests are linked to forming a "public identity" in universities that are all too often driven by a neo-liberal market logic.

Il-Hee Kim obtained a Ph.D. in Educational Psychology at the University of Illinois at Urbana-Champaign. He is an assistant professor in the College of Education and Public Policy at Indiana University-Purdue University Fort Wayne. His research on children's critical thinking skills has been published in major journals, including *American Educational Research Journal*, *Discourse Processes*, *Reading Research Quarterly*, and *Journal of the Learning Sciences*.

Jane M. Leatherman, Ph.D., received her degrees at the University of North Carolina at Greensboro in Early Childhood Special Education. Currently, she is the director of special education programs and associate professor at Indiana University-Purdue University Fort Wayne. Her research interests include collaboration among professionals in schools and best practices for inservice and preservice special education teachers. She has published in *Teaching Education* and the *Journal of Early Childhood Teacher Education*. She is a co-author of *An Administrator's Guidebook to Early Care and Education Programs*.

Ben Mardell is an associate professor in Early Childhood Education at Lesley University and a researcher on the Making Learning Visible Project at Project Zero at the Harvard Graduate School of Education. For the past 25 years, Ben has taught and conducted research with infants, toddlers, preschoolers and kindergartners. He is the author of *From Basketball to the Beatles: In Search of Compelling Early Childhood Curriculum* and *Growing Up in Child Care: A Case for Quality Early Education* and a co-author of *Making Learning Visible: Children as Individual and Group Learners* and *Making Teaching Visible: Documentation of Individual and Group Learning as Professional Development*.

Amber Merrill received her bachelor of arts in Education and her master of arts in Educational Psychology with a specialty in Gifted Education from Purdue University. She has been a gifted coordinator for youth programs with Purdue University, a school-wide gifted coordinator, an elementary classroom teacher, as well as a university adjunct instructor and a guest speaker focusing on the use of technology in the classroom. She has earned

Teacher of the Year, represented the State of Alabama at Congressional hearings concerning technology in the classroom, and worked on the development of mathematics instruction for the State of Alabama.

Alice Merz is an associate professor in the College of Education and Public Policy at Indiana University-Purdue University Fort Wayne. Dr. Merz's research focuses on case studies that examine how teachers become aware of and use interpretive lenses, such as the Reggio Approach, to guide their students' work, discourse, and dispositions. She teaches methods courses in elementary mathematics as well as graduate research methods courses.

Rebecca Newsome attended the University of North Carolina at Greensboro on a full Teaching Fellows Scholarship with the state of North Carolina. Rebecca graduated from UNCG with a bachelor of arts in Education degree majoring in Special Education. She is currently in her sixth year of teaching high school in the Exceptional Children's department at West Stokes High School in King, North Carolina.

Chris Strople taught for over 10 years in public elementary schools in southern California. He earned a B.A. in History from Loyola Marymount University, an M.A. in Teaching and also an M.A. in Educational Leadership and Administration from Chapman University. He is currently writing a doctoral dissertation and anticipates obtaining a Ph.D. in Cultural and Curricular Studies from Chapman University in 2012. His current research interests include understanding how identity and knowledge are formed and what impact that formation has on learning. His experiences as a classroom teacher were profoundly transformational and continue to inform his understanding of education.

Terri Jo Swim is an associate professor in Early Childhood Education at Indiana University-Purdue University Fort Wayne. Her research interests include curriculum for infants, toddlers, and preschoolers; Reggio-inspired practices, and the development of dispositions in children and teachers. She is the author or co-author of several publications including *Infants and Toddlers: Curriculum and Teaching* (7th Edition) and *Teacher National Accreditation as Community Dialogue: Transformative Reflections*.

Melissa Tonachel has been teaching young children for over 15 years, now at the Mission Hill K–8 School in Boston, where she also leads schoolwide professional development. She is a collaborating teacher with the Making Learning Visible Project at Project Zero at Harvard's Graduate School of Education. In addition, she recently began teaching graduate students at Lesley University, continuing her dedication to training new teachers in progressive, urban, public education. In fall 2012, the Mission Hill School will add two integrated classrooms of 3- and 4-year-olds and thus face the challenges outlined in our chapter.

Barry Kanpol
General Editor

The Critical Education and Ethics series intends to systematically analyze the pitfalls of social structures such as race, class, and gender as they relate to educational issues. Books in the series contain theoretical work grounded in pragmatic, society-changing practices. The series places value on ethical responses, as prophetic commitments to change the conditions under which education takes place.

The series aims to (1) Further the ethical understanding linking broader social issues to education by exploring the environmental, health-related, and faith/spiritual responses to our educational times and policy, and (2) Ground these works in the everyday world of the classroom, viewing how schools are impacted by what critical researchers do. Both theoretically and practically, the series aims to identify itself as an agent for community change.

The Critical Education and Ethics series welcomes work from emerging scholars as well as those already established in the field.

For additional information about this series or for the submission of manuscripts, please contact Dr. Kanpol (Indiana University—Purdue University Fort Wayne) at kanpolb@ipfw.edu.

To order other books in this series, please contact our Customer Service Department:

(800) 770-LANG (within the U.S.)
(212) 647-7706 (outside the U.S.)
(212) 647-7707 FAX

Or browse online by series at www.peterlang.com.